Is God Listening?

Is God Listening?

Making Prayer
a Part of Your Life

Andrew E. Steinmann

CONCORDIA PUBLISHING HOUSE · SAINT LOUIS

Published by Concordia Publishing House
3558 S. Jefferson Avenue, St. Louis, MO 63118–3968
Copyright © 2004 Andrew E. Steinmann

Scripture quotations are from the ESV Bible® (The Holy Bible, English Standard Version®), copyright © 2001 by Crossway Bibles, a publishing ministry of Good News Publishers. Used by permission. All rights reserved.

The quotation from the Large Catechism is from THE BOOK OF CONCORD: THE CONFESSIONS OF THE EVANGELICAL LUTHERAN CHURCH, edited by Robert Kolb and Timothy J. Wengert, copyright © 2000 Augsburg Fortress. Used by permission of Augsburg Fortress.

Library of Congress Cataloging-in-Publication Data

Steinmann, Andrew.
   Is God Listening? : making prayer a part of your life / Andrew E. Steinmann
     p. cm.
   ISBN 0-7586-0612-5
   1. Prayer—Christianity. I. Title
   BV210.3.S77 2004
   248.3′2—dc22

2 3 4 5 6 7 8 9 10 11   21 20 19 18 17 16 15 14 13 12

For everyone who prayed for me
and for all who prayed with me

✳ Contents

Preface

This book was written during a time that challenged me not only to pray but also to examine prayer. I had lost my job. The part-time jobs I found helped fill an economic need but left a spiritual void. I keenly felt that my God-given talents were not being used. I longed to have a job that would enable me to help provide for my family and also provide a meaningful way to use the talents I felt God had given me. In other words, I needed more than employment. I needed a vocation.

This need moved me to prayer. I prayed for many things, but above all else I prayed about my desire for a job that would be a vocation. At times it seemed as if God did not, could not, or would not hear my prayers. Although I was confident that He listened, I saw little tangible evidence of His attention to what I felt I needed the most.

Prayer had been a part of my life since childhood when my parents taught me to pray, showed me how to pray, and took me to church to pray. Yet the experience of prayer during this challenging period of my life has led me to a deeper appreciation of the privilege of prayer that God has given to His people. This book is a collection of my reflections and conclusions on some of the prayers in the Bible.

1

When God Seems Deaf

Prayer can feel like a lonely experience. Although some prayers are said in groups, before a meal, during worship, or before a meeting at church, prayer is often individual and private. We pray about our worries, fears, joys, needs, and wants. Such prayers are spontaneous, informal, unrehearsed thoughts brought to God.

When a concern dominates our thoughts for days or even weeks, we may find ourselves praying frequently about it. Such times are precisely when prayer seems to be a private and lonely experience. We have shared our most personal desires and thoughts with God, but we cannot see, feel, or hear God as we can our fellow believers. Talking to a close friend, a parent, a spouse, or even a therapist can have a healing effect because we receive instant feedback from the looks on their faces and their warm words. We may even receive a comforting embrace. Although God brings us the most comfort we could ever have, we receive none of those tangible, healing gestures that another believer can give us through a smile, hug, good laugh, or cry. Sometimes it bothers us when God does not seem to be here when we need that hug.

I have seen the lonely side of prayer in my work as a pastor at a nursing home. Many of the believers are confined to bed with little chance to do much, except perhaps watch television or listen to the radio. Residents spend a lot of time praying about their illnesses, their family and friends, and their desire that the Lord might take them to heaven soon. Yet every time I stopped by to visit with them, offer encouragement, and share God's Word, it seemed that the most special time was when we prayed together. They appreciated having a chance to pray with someone so much that they would often thank me for stopping by to *pray* with them. We may have talked, read the Bible, or shared some common interest, but praying with someone else seemed most important to them because it removed the loneliness from prayer.

On top of loneliness, we may feel as if God is not even hearing our prayers, let alone answering them. That is when the loneliness of prayer can be devastating. We feel as if we are lost in a wilderness without food or shelter, not knowing which way to turn and having no way of finding a path that will lead us out. When we feel as if we are praying to a God who doesn't hear, prayer seems emptied of its meaning and purpose. It seems as if God is deaf! Despair and hurt sometimes set in. Our will is seemingly crushed. But this is the wisdom of God as He teaches it. The believer's cross is at hand.

That is why we need to look at prayers in the Bible—especially prayers prayed by people who complained that God was not listening to them. We soon find that we are not alone in feeling that God is not paying attention. When we examine these prayers, we learn two things: First, prayer begins with God's promise of mercy toward us. Prayer does not begin with human effort to pester God until He listens. Second, prayer is designed to help us transcend our problems, our troubles, and our wills by focusing on God and His will. Prayer is not a way to manipulate God into answering all our questions or solving our problems in the ways we want them solved. This is why our focus is on God's Word, which teaches us to pray, and on the importance of the sacraments in the Christian's life.

Psalm 13—Confronting God in Prayer

How long, O LORD? Will You forget me forever?

How long will You hide Your face from me?

How long must I take counsel in my soul

and have sorrow in my heart all the day?

How long shall my enemy be exalted over me?

Consider and answer me, O LORD my God;

light up my eyes, lest I sleep the sleep

of death,

lest my enemy say, "I have prevailed over him,"

lest my foes rejoice because I am shaken.

But I have trusted in Your steadfast love;

my heart shall rejoice in Your salvation.

I will sing to the LORD,

because He has dealt bountifully with me.

In this prayer the psalmist boldly confronts his God who seems to be deaf and ignoring him. This is a prayer of desperation and trust, which may seem contradictory, but these emotions coexist in this prayer. The psalmist has lost hope and wonders whether God has permanently forgotten him. God has seemingly chosen to hide Himself from the psalmist. After all, God is not with him to give guidance or wise advice. In the psalmist's sorrow of feeling abandoned, he feels a need for guidance from heaven. Yet none is available. His prayers seem to go unanswered and unheard. The psalmist's hopelessness turns into desperation as he demands: "Look at me! Answer me!" He feels as if he is on the verge of death, and those who caused his tragic state will rejoice. The psalmist's enemies will have the joy of feeling they were right in doing whatever they did to make him miserable.

Psalm 13 could be prayed by any of us who feel we have been wronged by others who have gotten away with it. The utter hopelessness of feeling as if you have lost something unjustly at the hands of someone else with no way of getting it back is devastating. Whether you have lost your job, health, prosperity, friends, or family, the thought of never recovering what was lost can immobilize and paralyze the strongest of us. Television news reports often show a person who is grieving at the loss of a loved one. The grief of such people is almost too painful to watch as it is beamed into our homes. We know nothing will bring that lost loved one back. We can see the sorrow, rage, and gloom of the people crying over the deceased loved one. We are filled with their righteous anger and indignation as they call for justice to be done and the killers to be prosecuted and punished.

Although we can sympathize with such people as their stories are told to us through the flickering television screen, we cannot fully understand the depth of their emotions until we experience a similar loss. Whether that is a lost job, lost reputation, or lost friends, the grieving and hopelessness is strikingly similar to that experienced at the death of a loved one. At times these are multiple losses. Losing a job can mean losing the friends we had at work. Losing our reputation can cost us friends and perhaps even a job or a career.

When such a loss occurs, our prayers, like the psalmist's, can turn into cries of "How long?" How long is God going to allow me to suffer? Will this last for the rest of my life? Will I ever regain my job, reputation, friends, health, or prosperity? Often we know that what we have lost we have lost forever. The happy situation we knew cannot be reconstructed. Like Humpty Dumpty, nothing, not even all the king's horses and all the king's men, will ever put things back as they were. We often desire to have what we lost, but we know that is not what we will get.

However, notice that the psalmist's prayer was one of trust as well as hopelessness. Faith, or trust, brings hope. Faith always receives the strength and mercy that Christ gives. In faith, the psalmist accepts that everything that happens to him is under God's control (Romans 8:28). God could restore his position, his reputation, and his friends. But as much as the psalmist demands that God quit hiding and listen, he does not demand that God give him back what he lost. The psalmist's faith transcends his loss and grasps God's promises and refuses to let go.

God's mercy is the key to the psalmist's prayer. He admits he has no right to demand anything from God because God owes him nothing. Yet the psalmist knows that God will have mercy on him. The opponents who caused him loss and anguish may rejoice in overpowering him, but his joy is in God's salvation. Although it may not have been the salvation and vindication that the psalmist envisioned, he knows that God's plan or will to save him from his despair is best—whether or not it conforms to his own will.

The last line of this prayer is perhaps the most remarkable. The God who forgot the psalmist, the God who abandoned him to make decisions without spiritual guidance, is the God who has been good to the psalmist. Hopeless despair has turned into gratitude and praise. The desperate cries of a fallen man have become grateful songs. We see that God is beginning to answer the psalmist even before he is done praying. God promises to continue to be merciful to him. Not only did the psalmist receive his answer, but that answer began to change him before he got to his *amen*.

What Does God's Word Teach Us?

Psalm 13 teaches us our first important lesson about prayer: *Prayer begins with God's promise of mercy toward us. Prayer does not begin with a human effort to pester God until He listens.* The Bible does instruct us to pray often and always (Luke 18:1; 1 Thessalonians 5:17), but it does not tell us that God listens more closely simply because we pray more often (Matthew 6:7).

Prayer is not the same as calling God on the telephone and letting it ring over and over again until He answers us because He is tired of hearing the phone ring. Instead, prayer is our response to God's promise and gift of mercy to us. Because we know that He is merciful, that He forgives us and we are His dear children, we pray. Even when we think God is deaf and cannot or will not hear us, we trust His promise of mercy. God does not lie. In fact, God answered the psalmist's prayer by allowing him to realize God's mercy toward him even in the midst of the prayer.

The same mercy that the psalmist received is the same mercy God gives to us. The same faith or trust that the psalmist had in God's mercy is the same faith that God gave to us in our Baptism. God's mercy teaches us to pray. Yes, we pray even when we think God is deaf or ignoring us. In the end, we rejoice just like the psalmist because we trust that God is merciful and is as good to us as He was to the psalmist (see Luke 18:7–8). The psalmist trusts God and the work of our Lord Jesus Christ. Christ overcame sin, death, and the devil. He promises to give us strength to overcome our sorrows, losses, and tribulations.

☀ Psalm 77—Where Can We Find Comfort?

Another psalm in which someone called out for God to listen is Psalm 77. This prayer is attributed to Asaph, the musician David appointed to lead worship in the tabernacle. In this psalm the psalmist speaks of his inner feelings as he prays to God. This prayer can help us understand our feelings about praying to a seemingly deaf God.

> I cry aloud to God,
>
>> aloud to God, and He will hear me.
>
> In the day of my trouble I seek the Lord;
>
>> in the night my hand is stretched out
>>
>>> without wearying;
>>
>> my soul refuses to be comforted.
>
> When I remember God, I moan;
>
>> when I meditate, my spirit faints.
>>
>>> *Selah*

You hold my eyelids open;

    I am so troubled that I cannot speak.

I consider the days of old,

    the years long ago.

I said, "Let me remember my song in the night;

    let me meditate in my heart."

    Then my spirit made a diligent search:

"Will the Lord spurn forever,

    and never again be favorable?

Has His steadfast love forever ceased?

    Are His promises at an end for all time?

Has God forgotten to be gracious?

    Has He in anger shut up His compassion?"

                                Selah

Then I said, "I will appeal to this,

    to the years of the right hand of the

        Most High."

I will remember the deeds of the LORD;

    yes, I will remember Your wonders of old.

I will ponder all Your work,

    and meditate on Your mighty deeds.

Your way, O God, is holy.

    What god is great like our God?

You are the God who works wonders;

You have made known Your might among

the peoples.

You with Your arm redeemed Your people,

the children of Jacob and Joseph.

Selah

When the waters saw You, O God,

when the waters saw You, they were afraid;

indeed, the deep trembled.

The clouds poured out water;

the skies gave forth thunder;

Your arrows flashed on every side.

The crash of Your thunder was in the

whirlwind;

Your lightnings lighted up the world;

the earth trembled and shook.

Your way was through the sea,

Your path through the great waters;

yet Your footprints were unseen.

You led Your people like a flock

by the hand of Moses and Aaron.

This fascinating prayer expresses the emotional turmoil and pain that many people feel when they pray to God in the midst of trouble and cannot sense any response from Him. Although we do not know specifically what trouble this psalm is referring to, we know the psalmist went to God with it. Perhaps he had in mind the promise made by God in Psalm 50, another psalm of Asaph: "Call upon Me in the day of trouble; I will deliver you, and you shall glorify Me" (Psalm 50:15).

Whatever trouble the psalmist found himself in, this prayer reveals that it occupied all his thoughts. We do not know what the psalmist's friends and family thought of his preoccupation with his troubles. They may have been supportive; they may have thought it was silly. We have all had a similar experience. When something was troubling us, some friends advised us to talk to a counselor or our pastor. Others counseled us to forget the matter because it was not worth losing sleep over. (Notice that the psalmist said he was praying at night and his eyelids did not close.) Even if our trouble is not important to others, it is important to us. Sometimes we feel the only person we can go to with our trouble is to God.

God is exactly who the psalmist went to. He prayed with the normal posture of prayer in his day. Instead of folding his hands and bowing his head as we often do, he stretched out his arms and most likely looked upward toward heaven. In this position the psalmist shouted his prayer to God. His prayers must have been tiring, both physically and emotionally. It is not easy to keep our arms extended for long periods of time and even harder to do while we are speaking loudly. Yet the psalmist did not tire. He continued to stretch out his hands and pray.

Emotionally, God's seeming deafness to the psalmist's prayer was taking its toll. He had no inner comfort or peace that came as a result of his prayer. The psalmist speaks of losing hope and being so upset that he could no longer speak. Physically, he was able to stretch out his hands in prayer. However, he was so mentally and emotionally drained he couldn't sleep or voice his prayers out loud. The psalmist blames God for keeping his eyelids open and not bringing sleep. Perhaps the psalmist means that God was the cause of his insomnia because He was not answering his prayer (or at least by not answering it the way the psalmist desired).

When I was young, my cares and troubles rarely, if ever, kept me awake at night. I had little to worry about and even less to lose. As a child I was confident my parents would take care of my troubles. As a young man I had only myself to worry about. But as I grew older and took on the responsibilities of a husband and father, and as I was given the additional responsibilities of a job, I found that my troubles would keep me awake. I would fall asleep only to find myself wide awake in the middle of the night. I would toss and turn, and finally get up and try to forget my troubles by watching the feeble offerings of late-night television or by praying and meditating on the Bible. Often, like the psalmist, I could not speak my prayers out loud because I was so emotionally exhausted.

Because the psalmist was unable to sleep, his mind focused on what God had done for Israel. He remembered when he had joyfully sung to God during the night. Now, during this night of worry and distress, the psalmist searched back through God's relationship with His people and his own relationship with God. The psalmist wondered if these held the answers to his questions.

The psalmist's prayer is full of questions that must have run through his mind. Could he trust God to keep His promise of mercy? The psalmist implies that he had a preconceived notion of *how* God's mercy would affect his life. He not only wanted God's mercy but also His mercy to be shown in a certain way. If God would just do what the psalmist wanted and solve his difficulties in the way that the psalmist thought best, he would know God was merciful. Moreover, the psalmist's questions are signs of his impatience with God. When he asks if God will ever accept him, he is implying that he knows how God should solve his problem and when God should do it: *immediately!*

Many of the questions we have in times of trouble may not be the same questions that the psalmist asked. We usually want to know why God has allowed us to be in the situation we're in. One popular book published several years ago, *When Bad Things Happen to Good People*, sold many copies because we all want the answer to *why* such things happen. We especially want to know why bad things happen to us because we must be those good people the book title was speaking about. We ask ourselves: "Why is this happening to me? Why did God allow this to affect me (or someone I care about)?"

Notice that the psalmist never received an answer to his questions. He never tells us how or if God solved his problem. The psalm does not resolve his questions. It does not move him any closer to the time when his trouble will be solved. Often, our question of why something happened to us is never answered. Although we seek to know why God allows certain troubles to enter our life, knowledge itself will not solve our problems. Having an answer may not allow us to cope any better with them. Even if we could understand God's reasons for allowing certain difficulties to enter our lives, we would still need a solution to our troubles. Knowing why something happened will not comfort us, no matter how much we think it might.

What can comfort us? The psalmist was comforted when he remembered what God had done for His people in the past. Instead of using those ancient acts of God as a way to detect answers to the questions that plagued him, the psalmist found comfort in God's work with His people. The comfort was the answer to his prayer. The psalmist discovered that God led His people like a shepherd. Shepherds do not attempt to reason with their sheep. The sheep would not understand the answers if they had them. Sheep need wise leadership and protection, not answers. Sheep cannot fully understand what their shepherd does or why he does it. However, they can learn to trust the shepherd. (This insight alone can lead us to a greater appreciation of Psalm 23.)

When the psalmist reviewed Israel's history, he remembered God's miracles. He describes God's power at the Red Sea when He made a path through the raging waters. The people of Israel knew they were in trouble when the Egyptian armies were bearing down on them. They may have questioned why God put them in the trouble they found themselves in. They certainly thought they knew what was best for themselves and even provided a solution to their own problem (see Exodus 14:12). But they did not really know what was best. Had the children of Israel gotten their way, they would have remained enslaved. However, God's solution was provided through Aaron and Moses when the Red Sea parted and they crossed.

The psalmist recognized that his comfort came in trusting God's way of doing things. He rejoiced that God's ways are holy. He rejoiced that God created a path of escape through the sea for His people and did not let the sea collapse in on them. However, God's footprints could not be seen. As they moved toward the Red Sea, the children of Israel did not see evidence God was with them. They had to trust God was leading and would save them.

The New Testament shows us the work of God in the crucifixion of Jesus. Throughout Jesus' arrest, trial, and crucifixion we cannot see God's power forcefully at work. Instead, God, in the person of Jesus, appears to be at the mercy of the

Jewish leaders, the crowd, the Roman soldiers, and Pontius Pilate. The only footprints to follow are the footprints of a condemned man carrying a cross. God's power appears to be absent as Jesus is beaten, mocked, rejected, and dies a horrible death. The people at the foot of the cross taunt Jesus and remind Him that He said He trusted in God. Where was God to save Him now? (See Matthew 27:43.) Was God so deaf that He could not hear Himself? Was God deaf when Jesus cried out, "Eli, Eli, lema sabachthani?" that is, "My God, My God, why have You forsaken Me?" (Matthew 27:46)?

Yet the Bible makes clear that God was most active in the crucifixion of Christ. In this apparent display of weakness, God was leading His people out of death and sin just as He led them out of Egypt. The height of the glory of God is in this moment of sacrifice. The eyes see defeat, but faith sees victory and payment for our sin. God calls on us to trust Him. We trust that God saved us by the death of Jesus. The people of Israel had to trust that the sea would not collapse around them, that they would be led to freedom, not to their deaths. We are to trust that in the cross of Christ we are led to freedom from sin and death. And we are to trust that the same God who looked after His people at the Red Sea and in the death of Jesus is not deaf to our prayers.

Many see the death of Christ as the simple death of a man, maybe even the unjust death of a good man. But they do not see God at work in Jesus' death so they might be saved from slavery to sin and death. Like the Egyptians who followed the Israelites into the sea and were drowned, unbelievers cannot see what only the person who trusts God knows—that in Jesus' death He was at work to save His people. That same trust leads us to believe He is at work for us even when we think our prayers are falling on deaf ears. When God does not appear to be listening, He is still working for us. In prayer we focus on God, and we are reminded to trust Him even when we cannot see His footprints.

The psalmist's comfort, then, was not from God answering all his questions or by solving his problems in the way he thought God should solve them. The psalmist's comfort was found in God Himself. God was the answer to his prayer. The psalmist learned to trust his shepherd.

Psalm 77 teaches us a second important lesson about prayer: *Prayer is designed to help us transcend our problems and troubles by focusing on God Himself. Prayer is not a way to manipulate God into answering all our questions or solving our problems in the ways we want them solved.* When it seems that God is deaf to our prayers, it is we who are unable to hear or understand. God appears deaf to our prayers because we do not want to be sheep that trust the shepherd. We must remember that our shepherd knows more than we can understand. God's deafness is really our lack of trust in the One who has the power to defend His people and control the water, the clouds, the sky, thunder and lightning, the death of His Son, and the events in our life. When God's Word teaches us to pray, we learn to pray and focus on who God really is and what He has done. It allows us to transcend our troubles even when God appears to be deaf.

>—+—◦—+—<

In this chapter I have touched on only two prayers in the Bible. In both prayers the child of God was desperate for an answer from Him. The psalmists felt that God seemed to be deaf to their prayers. However, God answered them through His own deeds as they confessed God's actions, mercy, and salvation.

For further meditation, you may want to read Psalm 10, 22, 44, 88, and 89. A number of psalms ask God not to hide from those who pray them and beg God not to be deaf. These psalms do not exhibit the hopelessness of those who prayed the prayers examined in this chapter. Nevertheless, such psalms can also teach us about praying when God seems to be ignoring us (see Psalm 28).

2

When Evil Is Winning

In A.D. 410 the Goth Alaric and his army conquered and sacked the city of Rome. For many Christians, this was a calamity without equal. The great Roman Empire that had been such an enemy of the church in its formative years officially became Christian, and the emperors converted to Christianity. Now the pagan Goths had conquered Rome's empire. Many non-Christians in Rome blamed its fall on the Christian religion. Not only did it seem that evil from outside of Rome was winning but also that evil inside the city was vexing the church. In the midst of all this, Augustine, bishop of Hippo in North Africa, wrote *The City of God*. In this book Augustine argues that no human city or government should be equated with God, His church, or with victory over evil. Cities built by humans will pass away, Augustine argued, but God's eternal city, the New Jerusalem, is the hope of Christians even when evil seems to overcome the good in this life.

Augustine's answer to evil is good, but hard to accept if you are experiencing the effects of evil directly. It was probably easy for Augustine to write his book from a distance as he looked at Rome. However, the Roman Christians, though they knew in their hearts that Augustine was right, had to cope day-to-day with the evil that had come upon them. They were confronted by the evil around them that seemed to be triumphing over good. They chaffed under its apparent victory and often resented that the pagan hordes were now their masters and, in some cases, their tormentors.

Sixteen centuries later, we can look back on the fall of Rome and see that evil did not triumph over the church. The church survived. Yet when something evil happens to us or those whom we care about, we have a much harder time seeing the big picture. In the midst of our sufferings, it is hard to trust that God will work them out for our good. In our sinful state, we always want to know, "Why?" Why does evil seem to win? We may even pray that God would punish those who did the evil and rescue us from our pain and despair.

Prayer is a proper way to confront the problem of evil in the world. In this chapter we will consider three types of prayers that we can pray in response to evil when it touches our lives: (1) We can pray that God would punish those who do evil. (2) We can pray that God will bless us when we avoid evil and try to do good. (3) We can pray for those who do evil. We turn now to read prayers from the Bible wherein someone experienced the consequences of someone else's evil deeds. From these prayers we will learn two lessons: First, we can ask God to deal with evil, even to punish evil people. However, it is wrong for us to expect God to make the result be one in which we can see that good unambiguously triumphs over evil. Second, our prayers can be proactive. They can ask God for blessings and for good to come from what we do.

✳ Psalm 137—"Dear God, Punish Those Who Do Evil"

By the waters of Babylon,

   there we sat down and wept,

   when we remembered Zion.

On the willows there we hung up our lyres.

For there our captors

   required of us songs,

and our tormentors, mirth, saying,

   "Sing us one of the songs of Zion!"

How shall we sing the LORD's song

   in a foreign land?

If I forget you, O Jerusalem,

   let my right hand forget its skill!

Let my tongue stick to the roof of my mouth,

   if I do not remember you,

if I do not set Jerusalem

   above my highest joy!

Remember, O LORD, against the Edomites

   the day of Jerusalem,

how they said, "Lay it bare, lay it bare,

   down to its foundations!"

O daughter of Babylon, doomed to be
destroyed,
blessed shall he be who repays you
with what you have done to us!
Blessed shall he be who takes your little ones
and dashes them against the rock!

The first Judeans who prayed this psalm were bitter. Their homeland was attacked, overrun, and conquered by the Babylonians, a ruthless, destructive people, and the Judeans were forced to leave their land and live in exile. Similar things have occurred to many people in this century and television documents the suffering in painful detail. We have seen refugees so numerous they strain even the most up-to-date means of providing humanitarian aid. During the siege of Judah's capital city, Jerusalem, many watched in horror as their children and elderly starved to death or slowly wasted away from disease. We have also seen scenes of children with bloated, empty stomachs. Too often they are innocent victims of war or a ruthless, unjust government or dictator.

However, comparisons of the Judeans' experience to our own tend to fade when we consider the other things they suffered at the hands of the Babylonians. The Israelites were forced to live in the land of their conquerors, the very people who destroyed their land, enslaved them, and killed their families. Moreover, their captors mocked them by demanding, "Sing a song of Zion for us." We might think that this request is a small thing. But to those who first prayed Psalm 137, it was a terrible religious insult.

To understand why this was an insult let us learn more about the religious nature of ancient warfare in the Middle East. When a king went to war, he believed that his god went with him and fought beside him against the opposing king's god. A king's victory would also be his god's victory. The victory was proof of who was the superior god. Often, the conquered people were forced to adopt the conquering god as their own.

Against this background, the people of Judah were faithful to their God. They acknowledged and worshiped only one God—the God of their ancestors Abraham, Isaac, and Jacob, the God of Moses, and their greatest king, David. No other god existed. Yet the Babylonians claimed their god had defeated Israel's God. Therefore, the Babylonian god was declared superior. Many Judeans refused to admit the supremacy of the Babylonian god. The Judeans confessed their God in the face of the whole world. They went against the popular religious war beliefs of the day. So they suffered ridicule at the hands of the Babylonians who mocked the Judeans and demanded that they, "Sing a song about Zion." This insult was a way of telling the Judeans that their God was unable to defend them and their city.

The pain and humiliation became even worse. Judah's neighbor Edom had joined the Babylonians in destroying Jerusalem. They cheered for its destruction. The descendants of Jacob's brother, Esau, who had sold his birthright and despised God's blessing, triumphed with the Babylonians. The evil of the Babylonians had prevailed. The evils of their warfare had reduced Judah to rubble and its people to oppression. The god of Babylon appeared to be spiritually superior. How were the Judeans to pray under these circumstances? What were they to ask of God? What would we pray if we were to face seeming defeat of our God?

How could the Judeans sing about Zion, the great city of their God, under such bitter conditions? How could they sing with the joy they use to have? Yet the Judeans were determined to not forget their God and the joy of worshiping Him in Jerusalem. The Judean's bitterness would not keep them from singing to Him. The taunts of their captors would not dim their faith in the one true God, the one they had worshiped on Mount Zion.

The Judeans prayed: "O daughter of Babylon, doomed to be destroyed, blessed shall he be who repays you with what you have done to us! Blessed shall he be who takes your little ones and dashes them against the rock!" (Psalm 137:8–9). This request is emotionally understandable, but because it is in the Bible it might seem shocking to us. How could this violent request be in the same Bible as the advice: "Love your enemies and pray for those who persecute you" (Matthew 5:44)? Is this a proper prayer when evil and evildoers triumph in this world?

When evil wins, something seems terribly wrong. Perhaps the hardest time to pray is when we have been wronged by immoral actions. It angers us when we see a morally wrong nation prevail over a nation that did what was right. In books, movies, and on television our sense of morality is played out time and again. The good guys usually win the ultimate victory and are vindicated in the end. Sometimes they even win in real life. But many times it is the ruthless and immoral use of power and authority that wins. At times that power resides in those who bend and break every moral law but remain smugly self-righteous about themselves and their actions. Some get away with their immoral acts without ever paying a price for them. Others pay a price that is insignificant compared to the pain and misery they brought to others.

When we see evil triumph in our world, we can understand why the Judeans placed a blessing on those who paid back the Babylonians for their evil. Our sense of moral outrage at the triumph of evil causes us to cry out for the punishment of the evildoer. We rejoice in the evildoer's suffering as much as the Judeans who prayed that someone would smash Babylon's children against a rock. But even as we rejoice, the thought persists that such calls for vengeance may also be evil. How do we pray in these circumstances? Is there a difference between a just reward for evil and revenge for evil? Let's move on and see who else has prayed for vengeance in the Bible.

✳ Jeremiah and Habakkuk— Prophets Who Prayed for Vengeance

Many prayers in the Bible call on God to punish those who have done something evil toward the person praying. When some men plotted to assassinate Jeremiah, he prayed:

> But, O LORD of hosts, who judges righteously,
>
> who tests the heart and the mind,
>
> let me see Your vengeance upon them,
>
> for to You have I committed my cause.
>
> *(11:20)*

On other occasions Jeremiah prayed:

> Let those be put to shame who persecute me,
>   but let me not be put to shame;
> let them be dismayed,
>   but let me not be dismayed;
> bring upon them the day of disaster;
>   destroy them with double destruction!
>   *(17:18)*

In perhaps his most powerful prayer for vengeance, Jeremiah prayed:

> Hear me, O Lord,
>   and listen to the voice of my adversaries.
> Should good be repaid with evil?
>   Yet they have dug a pit for my life.
> Remember how I stood before You
>   to speak good for them,
>   to turn away Your wrath from them.
> Therefore deliver up their children to famine;
>   give them over to the power of the sword;
> let their wives become childless and widowed.
>   May their men meet death by pestilence,
>   their youths be stuck down by the sword
>   in battle.

May a cry be heard from their houses,

    when You bring the plunderer suddenly

      upon them!

For they have dug a pit to take me

    and laid snares for my feet.

Yet You, O Lord, know

    all their plotting to kill me.

Forgive not their iniquity,

    nor blot out their sin from Your sight.

Let them be overthrown before You;

    deal with them in the time of

      Your anger.

(18:19–23)

Jeremiah's prayers ask God to severely punish those who tried to harm him. He wants God to terrify them, to destroy them, to punish their wives, husbands, and children, and to refuse them any forgiveness. Jeremiah is not alone in praying that God would undo the triumphant evil that harmed him. David prayed that God would make it possible for him to defeat Absalom (2 Samuel 15:31). Nehemiah prayed that God would not forget what his enemies had done (Nehemiah 6:14) and that God would not forget the sins of the priests who had brought dishonor on their holy office (Nehemiah 13:29). These are precisely the type of prayers we, too, are tempted to pray when someone harms us. These prayers are especially attractive when we know that our harm is undeserved because we did nothing wrong.

This fervor in calling for punishment for those who wronged others can be seen in the continuing outrage against surviving Nazis and Nazi collaborators from World War II. The atrocities committed in Germany took place over sixty years ago. Most of those who worked with the Nazis have died, and those who are still alive are elderly. Yet several governments still spend time and money to seek out and prosecute the few frail old people who committed those wicked deeds two generations ago. It is hard to give up the desire for vengeance—even after half a century—in the face of terrible and unspeakable crimes that were committed against innocent people. Is it any wonder, then, that we also cling to vengeful emotions for injustices done to us personally?

Is it wrong to pray that God would execute justice against evil and those who do it, especially when evil appears to be winning? Is it improper to pray that God would punish evil? Should we refrain from praying about vengeance for the evil that has touched our lives? If we answer yes to any of these questions, we probably have to remove the book of Habakkuk from our Bibles. Habakkuk records three of his prayers asking God to punish those who do evil things. The first is Habakkuk 1:2–4:

> O Lord, how long shall I cry for help,
>
>   and You will not hear?
>
> Or cry to You "Violence!"
>
>   and You will not save?
>
> Why do You make me see iniquity,
>
>   and why do You idly look at wrong?

Destruction and violence are before me;

strife and contention arise.

So the law is paralyzed,

and justice never goes forth.

For the wicked surround the righteous;

so justice goes forth perverted.

In this prayer Habakkuk asks God why evil is allowed to triumph. The prophet was concerned that many good people were suffering because of the wrongdoing that was allowed to take place in his society. Habakkuk's prayer also points out another consequence of God's inaction: God's Word, His teachings to His people, is ignored. Apparently, some people in Judah felt it was pointless to live according to God's teachings because evil was going to win anyway. Why bother to try to be good?

God answered Habakkuk's prayer. God revealed to Habakkuk that He would use the Babylonians as His instrument to punish the evil deeds of Judah (Habakkuk 1:6–7). But this raised another problem for Habakkuk. Weren't the Babylonians committing their own kind of evil? So Habakkuk prayed again:

Are You not from everlasting,

O LORD my God, my Holy One?

We shall not die.

O LORD, You have ordained them as a

judgment,

and You, O Rock, have established them
    for reproof.
You who are of purer eyes than to see evil
    and cannot look at wrong,
why do You idly look at traitors
    and are silent when the wicked swallows up
    the man more righteous than he?
You make mankind like the fish of the sea,
    like crawling things that have no ruler.
He brings all of them up with a hook;
    he drags them out with his net;
he gathers them in his dragnet;
    so he rejoices and is glad.
Therefore he sacrifices to his net
    and makes offerings to his dragnet;
for by them he lives in luxury,
    and his food is rich.
Is he then to keep on emptying his net
    and mercilessly killing nations forever?
                    (1:12–17)

God's answer to Habakkuk did not solve his problem. If anything, the answer made things worse. He still thought evil would triumph over good in the world, but in a different way. Habakkuk knows that God cannot even look at evil. How could God use one evil to punish another? The Babylonians were a worse evil according to Habakkuk. They were conquerors who showed no mercy to people. They were idolaters who did terrible things to people who were more righteous than they. Now God was going to use them to punish the evil people in Judah. To Habakkuk this didn't seem like much of a solution. Habakkuk even said that to God in his second prayer.

The answer Habakkuk received reaffirmed God's decision to use Babylon to punish the evil in Judah. The prophet wrote:

And the LORD answered me:

"Write the vision;

make it plain on tablets,

so he may run who reads it.

For still the vision awaits its appointed time;

it hastens to the end—it will not lie.

If it seems slow, wait for it;

it will surely come; it will not delay."

(2:2–3)

God continues with a promise to Habakkuk that He will punish evil people: those who are arrogant (2:4–6a); those who become rich by dishonest means (2:6b–8); those who use violence to attain what they want (2:9–11); those who gain political strength through criminal activity (2:12–14); those who involve others in their wicked acts and bring God's anger on them (2:15–17); and those who worship idols (2:19). God will see that all of them are punished in some way. Therefore, even though He will use the wicked Babylonians to punish others, the Babylonians will be punished as well.

What was the conclusion for the prophet? "The Lord is in His holy temple; let all the earth keep silence before Him" (Habakkuk 2:20). Habakkuk realized that God is holy and cannot tolerate evil. God remains holy and from His holy temple He deals with evil. None on earth can question God's solution to the problem of evil. We must let God be God. There is much in God's will that He does not reveal to us on purpose. It is often called the hidden will of God. What He does reveal is that He is holy. The details of how He will deal with evil in daily life are hidden.

Here we come to the first lesson about praying to God to punish evil: *It is not wrong to ask God to deal with evil, even to punish evil people. However, it is wrong to expect God to make the result be one in which humans can see that good unambiguously triumphs over evil.* The problem of evil in this world is much more complicated than we humans can comprehend. It runs deep in every culture, every life, every day. Everything in life we value as good is complicated by the evil that lies deep in humans (see Romans 3:9–19). Considering the pervasive nature of evil and how closely it is tied to everything we do, we really cannot expect a simple "good will triumph in the end" answer to our prayers about evil. We can only trust that God does deal with evil because He said He would. He alone comprehends the widespread web of evil in the world. It is not our place to judge how God deals with evil on a daily basis.

We may not even recognize God's answer to our prayers. Would Habakkuk have recognized the answer to his prayer about the evil in Judah if God had not revealed it to him? His reaction shows that he would not have. Our attitude today is that we want quick, simple, and straightforward solutions to all our problems. We tend to think in terms of the sitcom that will solve a problem and bring a family back together in

22 minutes of airtime. We enjoy the speed and immediacy of the Internet. Should I have a question about a car I want to buy, I have a series of answers in 15 minutes—no more waiting two to four days for letters to arrive in the mail. With chat rooms and e-mail, an electronic conversation can take place in 10 minutes with someone on the other side of the country without a phone.

Another sign of our attitude can be seen in the way we now look for news. It was not long ago that we waited all day for the evening news. Now, with 24-hour news coverage, we expect to turn on the television any time, day or night, and get the information we want on any news item of the day. Once again we expect immediate and speedy access to answers.

But can we really believe that news stories on television, even if they are on all day and all night, do anything more than scratch the surface of the problems? Is it the fault of the media that when a television or radio program devotes twenty minutes or an hour to one story it is considered in-depth coverage? When we make use of the answers on the Internet or take advantage of the high speed of communication through e-mail, do we think that all communication should be done this way? Is this the best way to deal with marriage problems and the intimacies of a relationship? There is always more to a relationship than quick communication.

As Christians, we must understand the role of sin in all of our high-speed attitudes. Certainly, it is not necessarily wrong to use the Internet, send e-mail, or watch television. But what role does sin and evil play in our desire for quick and speedy solutions to our problems? Do we have the patience to grasp how evil has complicated our world? Is patience an important virtue anymore? How often is it that we don't want to take the time to understand the real root of our problems?

The speed of the Internet and the immediacy of 24-hour news programs are issues we deal with in our lives, yet they are not earth-shattering problems. On the other hand, when we pray to God about a serious problem, what do we expect? Do we evaluate His answers based upon our experience with television or the Internet? Will God answer our problems with the quick results like those from a search engine in a web browser? Are we are even more impatient and shortsighted with God?

When we approach the throne of God, we approach His holiness. Sin is the problem with evil. Sin is the problem with our problems. Sin permeates all that we think and do. Our finest deeds are not even close to the holiness of God. It is no wonder that we often miss it when God answers our prayers and deals with evil and evil people. His solutions deal with the intricacies and complications of life as a result of sin. God offers the right solution that He knows is best for us, not what we think is best for us. We often cannot comprehend God's answers to our prayers. He alone can see the intricacies of our lives, our relationships, our hurts, and our real needs. He is God. He alone can put this whole puzzle together, in spite of our sin. He forgives our sin. Through faith in Christ, we are holy. As holy people of God, the holy God will give holy answers for our good.

Habakkuk learned that God's answer to his prayer about evil was to be accepted. His prayer accepts God's solutions to the presence of evil in the world.

O Lord, I have heard the report of You,

and Your work, O Lord, do I fear.

In the midst of the years revive it;

in the midst of the years make it known;

in wrath remember mercy.

(3:2)

Throughout this prayer Habakkuk displays a healthy fear and respect for God's power because God used His power to act against evil. Habakkuk now understands that sometimes the people or things God uses to punish evil in this world can bring suffering, pain, and even death. Habakkuk prays that God will reveal His work so it can be seen and appreciated. He prays that God will continue to do His work and to renew it as the years run their course. From this prayer we can see God's use of suffering and death to bring justice, time, and the ability to see the work of God revealed.

However, we want answers now! Actually, we usually want answers yesterday. However, time brings insight, wisdom, and respect. As we mature in our prayers, we realize the importance of time. How often has it been that when we prayed, we thought we saw an answer that was what we wanted, but then realized it wasn't? How do you know that was God's answer? You don't. That's why we trust God to do His will, not ours. To begin to grasp God's will we need to take time to be patient and mature, which takes years to do. Habakkuk, in his maturity, prayed that God would reveal His answer "in the midst of the years." God promises to care for us, to watch out for us, and to be merciful to us. He even died for us! God promises to answer our prayers in the course of years in a way that will be merciful to us and teach us to respect His will, especially when we see suffering, injustice, and destruction. We don't need to see the work of God except for what He reveals in His Word. Often, only in hindsight, are we able to see how God put things together for our good. Rarely, if ever, do we "see" God's will in our daily lives while we go through suffering, temptation, and pain. God's will is clear in His Word, but the details of His daily work is God's business, not ours. We are certain only of the promises of God. For the details of our daily life God gives us the freedom to live and pray "Thy will be done," especially in the midst of suffering. God's will is always better than our will.

Finally, Habakkuk prays that God will remember to be merciful. When God used the Babylonians to punish evil, Habakkuk saw many people suffer. He prays that suffering would be limited by God's mercy. Habakkuk came to respect God's power and his prayer is now more mature. He wants God to use His power to punish wickedness. At the same time, Habakkuk recognizes God could punish all people for their failings. So he now prays God would remember to be merciful. He teaches us that when we pray for God to reverse evil's triumph over good, we also ask God to temper His anger with mercy so that we do not all perish. When our prayer for God to deal with evil in the world or specific evils that touch our lives becomes a mature prayer, we will be able to pray as Habakkuk did. We will pray for God's will to be done when we are under attack, for God to be merciful to our enemies, when we face death, and in the pain of hunger. Habakkuk prayed:

> Though the fig tree should not blossom,
>   nor fruit be on the vines,
> the produce of the olive fail
>   and the fields yield not food,
> the flock be cut off from the fold

and there be no herd in the stalls,

yet I will rejoice in the LORD;

I will take joy in the God of my salvation.

GOD, the Lord, is my strength;

He makes my feet like the deer's;

He makes me tread on my high places.

(3:17–19)

 ## Nehemiah and the Apostles— Praying for Blessing When Beset by Evil

Is calling on God to punish evil the only attitude we should adopt when we pray? Or do alternatives to the type of prayers prayed by the Judeans, Jeremiah, and Habakkuk exist? One alternative is found in the Book of Nehemiah. Nehemiah not only prayed that God would remember those who did evil things (Nehemiah 6:14; 13:29) but also that God would remember the good that he did.

> "Remember for my good, O my God, all that I have done for this people."
>
> *(5:19)*

> "Remember me, O my God, concerning this, and do not wipe out my good deeds that I have done for the house of my God and for His service."
>
> *(13:14)*

> "Remember this also in my favor, O my God, and spare me according to the greatness of Your steadfast love."
>
> *(13:22b)*

"Remember me, O my God, for good."

(13:31b)

Nehemiah did pray that God would punish the evil actions of those who opposed his work for God's people or who disregarded God's Word and the welfare of His people. But these prayers show that Nehemiah's primary response to evil's seeming triumph in the world was to ask God to bless him and his work. Nehemiah focused his prayers against evil on the good God could accomplish through him. Instead of merely praying God would punish evil, he prayed God would reward good. This is another way of confronting triumphant evil in the world. Nehemiah confronted evil through action and prayed God would bless him for the good he did, and that God would allow the good he did to flourish.

Here we have a second lesson about praying when evil appears to be winning: *Our prayers can be proactive. They can ask God for blessings and for good to come from what we do.* In this way, our prayers can be answered as God moves us to action. Instead of being immobilized by evil that appears to dominate and win, we can pray that God will bless our actions so they are forces for good. Nehemiah was opposed by some powerful men who intended to use their power to harm his people. Those powerful and wicked men did not stop Nehemiah from doing good. Instead, he prayed God would continue to make him an agent that would accomplish something beneficial for others.

The rage we feel when evil triumphs over good can paralyze us. Nehemiah's prayers show us that there is an alternative to that paralysis. We can pray that God would move us to do what is right and beneficial for others. We can pray that God would bless us and reverse the effects of evil in our lives.

Such prayers are not self-centered prayers that only benefit us. Rather, they are prayers that teach us how to combat evil in the world by using the blessings God gives us.

The apostles prayed the same type of prayer when the authorities in Jerusalem threatened them. They prayed:

> Sovereign Lord, who made the heaven and the earth and the sea and everything in them, who through the mouth of our father David, Your servant, said by the Holy Spirit,
>
> "Why did the Gentiles rage,
>
> and the peoples plot in vain?
>
> The kings of the earth set themselves,
>
> and the rulers were gathered together,
>
> against the Lord and against His Anointed"—
>
> for truly in this city there were gathered together against Your holy servant Jesus, whom You anointed, both Herod and Pontius Pilate, along with the Gentiles and the peoples of Israel, to do whatever Your hand and Your plan had predestined to take place. And now, Lord, look upon their threats and grant to Your servants to continue to speak Your word with all boldness, while You stretch out Your hand to heal, and signs and wonders are performed through the name of Your holy servant Jesus.
>
> *(Acts 4:24–30)*

The wicked authorities did not paralyze the apostles. They did not cause the apostles to ask God to punish the authorities. Instead, the apostles prayed that God would use them to accomplish good and overcome the evil the authorities had in mind. Such prayers are prayers of faith and trust that God can use us, even when we are oppressed by the evil done by others.

✳ Stephen: Praying for Those Who Do Evil

A third possible response to evil is found in Acts 7:59–60. As Stephen was being stoned by council members, "he called out, 'Lord Jesus, receive my spirit.' And falling to his knees he cried out with a loud voice, 'Lord, do not hold this sin against them.' And when he had said this, he fell asleep."

Stephen's prayer is perhaps the most difficult response to evil for us to understand. The injustice of evil makes it easy for us to be angry. It is easy to ask God to punish those who commit crimes and are wicked. It is not uncommon to see relatives of someone murdered calling for the punishment and even execution of those who are accused of committing the murder. It is normal and even proper for the sake of a good community to bring justice and appropriate punishment for unjust deeds. We certainly expect the authorities to do their work. But is that the same as wanting God to provide the "pay backs" against the unjust? What do we want to see done in our hearts? We know we want to strike back when someone strikes us. So would we pray faithfully for God to be merciful to those who act unjustly toward us? Would you dare to forgive them even as they act against you? When Stephen prayed, he asked God to overlook the sins of those who were murdering him. How can we find the compassion in our hearts to pray like that? Where can we find the resources to ask God to overlook or forgive the willfully wicked acts of people who simply do not care whether they are on the side of evil?

Perhaps it would be easier to pray as Jesus did from the cross: "Father, forgive them, for they know not what they do" (Luke 23:34). We could possibly find a way to pray for those who commit some evil act against us if we thought that they did not realize the gravity of what they were doing. But in Stephen's case, his killers knew what they were doing. They refused to listen to what Stephen had to say and were intent on killing him (Acts 7:57). Yet, even then, Stephen asked God not to hold their sin against them. Such prayers take human compassion beyond what we expect of even the best people.

The key to being able to pray this type of prayer in the face of cruelest evil is to understand the will of God as He reveals it in His Word. We learn how to pray from what Stephen saw while his enemies stoned him to death. St. Luke tells us that Stephen saw God's glory in heaven. Jesus was standing in the position of authority at God's right side (Acts 7:55). As we learned in the previous chapter, a Christian prayer focuses on God and His work. Stephen was focused on God and saw His glory. The will of God is the will of Jesus. The glory of God is the glory of Jesus. How did Jesus finally return to His glory and authority? What was the cup from which Jesus drank to reach the right hand of God? He drank from the cup of suffering—the wrath of God on the cross. Jesus was abandoned to hell to pay for our sin. The glory of God is in the suffering and the cross. Even now, we participate in heaven and the glory of God by faith in Christ and His promises. Like Stephen, our earthly reality is suffering, pain, and eventual death. Christ teaches us how to suffer and even die. The vision of Christ for Stephen is no different than the vision of Christ in our lives. Our lives still endure the pain and suffering of sin. Not until we die do we fully experience heaven and the eternal glory of God. Now we live in God's mercy, enduring our crosses. We fully rely on the work of Jesus to bring us forgiveness and peace.

The glory Stephen saw was the heavenly reality. Where Jesus is, there is heaven. Jesus brought forgiveness to everyone who is in heaven and there He rules with all power and authority. Yet here on earth Jesus still rules in humility until the end of the world. The humility of His rule on earth is for our own good, for we can read the Word. For us Jesus governs in the lowliness of the glory of forgiveness in the waters of Baptism. Heaven comes to us in His body and blood in the bread and wine of the Lord's Supper.

Stephen could pray for the pardon of his killers because he knew that he had God's forgiveness. He saw the glory of God in the death of Jesus. He saw God's will unfold before his eyes. Stephen could leave the punishment for his own death in Jesus' hands. He could concentrate on the glory of God that we all can see in the forgiveness God gives us. That is why God teaches us to focus our prayer on Him. When God is the focus of prayer, He provides us with the compassion to pray for those who do many of the terrible, evil acts in the world.

>—+—‹›—O—‹•—+—◃

Moses' prayer to God in Numbers 11:10–15 is another example of prayer in response to wickedness. Many of the psalms address this problem as one of their major themes. Among them are Psalm 3–5, 7, 11, 12, 14, 17, 30, 31, 35, 43, 54–56, 58, 59, 62, 64, 69–71, 73, 74, 86, 94, 109, 129, and 140. When evil seems to be winning or when you are outraged at the immorality of others who have hurt you, pray and focus on God who alone conquers sin and evil.

3

When Sin Is Recognized

Guilt is a powerful emotion that can cause us to alter our behavior. Some people feel so guilty about something they have done they will go out of their way to avoid the person they have harmed. Others go out of their way to be nice to those whom they hurt. A child may be especially nice to a parent, or a spouse may buy a special gift for his or her partner because of guilt.

I knew a man who was in charge of a small organization. He had one serious flaw: He was jealous when those under him succeeded. He didn't want to share any credit with them and felt as if he was being kept out of the spotlight when they were praised for their work. Often he would deny them opportunities to work on projects that they would have found rewarding as a way of keeping them from outshining his performance. When they proposed ideas to solve problems or offered insights that could have kept the organization from making costly errors, he would ignore them and berate their ideas. On their annual evaluations he would rate them poorly, even though they had accomplished much, or shuffle them off to another position. Sometimes he would even demote them or fire them. This way he would not have to share the glory with others or admit that his decisions caused the problems to begin with.

Needless to say, this was not good for morale. Nor was it good for the supervisor's conscience. He would try to win back the employee's favor by buying lunch or making a promise of some perk. However, the promises often went unfulfilled. At other times he would give pep talks and tell the employees what great accomplishments they were achieving, all the while implying that he was the main reason that they were accomplishing anything—even when he had made the mistakes. Sometimes the pep talks would turn into ways of defending the organization's failed policies when often he was the one who set them up. The pep talks could even transform themselves into opportunities for reminding the employees of their unspeakable sin of trying to offer suggestions for improvements.

But this behavior did not win back the employees' favor and boost morale. It was merely a way of covering up his guilt, and the employees knew it. Instead of having the effect he intended, his behavior deepened his feelings of guilt and further alienated the workers. His temporary change in behavior was no substitute for facing his guilt and admitting that he had harmed others to satisfy his own ego.

Behavior is not the only thing that can change when someone is feeling guilty. Our attitude can also change. We can blame the people we harmed and attempt to convince ourselves it was their fault, not ours (like the supervisor's bad performance evaluations of his employees). If that does not seem to be a good avenue to escape our guilt, we can deny what we did. We can deny our guilt even to the point where we convince ourselves that we did not do what we actually did. In extreme cases, some people have become pathological liars because of guilt. They deny the truth so easily that they believe their own lies. In less extreme cases, people engage in a kind of personal revision of history, redefining their actions in ways that convince them that what they have done was harmless or even beneficial for others (like the supervisor's self-serving pep talks).

Another strategy used by people to cope with guilt is redefining what is right and what is wrong. One way this is done is by equating what is legally allowable with what is ethically and morally right. At other times people simply deny that there can be any absolute moral code by which we should all live. Personal opinion on right and wrong is all that matters. Guilt is gone because no standard can be used to make us feel guilty.

All of these ways of coping with guilt usually create more problems than they solve. If we are nice to someone because we feel guilty, they may resent us even more. They may want us to be nice to them sincerely, not because we are trying to work ourselves into their good graces. Or they may take advantage of our guilt and use it to get what they want. In either case, we do not get what we are really trying to obtain—a renewed relationship. If we resort to blaming others or denying to ourselves what we have done, we develop unhealthy behavior. That behavior could lead us to make more mistakes in the future and even into self-destructive behavior. If we hide behind the law or behind an attitude that believes no objective standard of behavior can govern our lives, we can hardly complain when others harm us. When we choose one of these ways of coping with guilt, we choose to avoid solving our problem.

However, the Bible offers us a real solution to the problem of guilt. Instead of tying to cope with guilt, we can pray as God's Word teaches us to pray. Many prayers in the Bible focus on the solution of *recognizing our guilt and admitting that we are wrong.* For many people, this is the most difficult way to deal with guilt. The mechanisms we have for handling guilt are ways of trying to save ourselves the embarrassment and uncomfortable feelings that come with admitting we have done something that is morally or ethically wrong. We want to escape the feeling that we have harmed someone. Although our ways of coping with guilt may seem like an escape, they can cause more complications for our lives. The Bible's solution, though uncomfortable, solves the problem of guilt.

As we examine some prayers in the Bible that were spoken by people who admitted their wrongs and recognized their guilt, we will discover three important truths:

First, prayers of confession should neither be prayed as an easy way out of our guilt nor as a way to escape the negative consequences of sin. Prayers of confession are prayed because we trust God's promise of forgiveness.

Second, true prayers of confession are also prayers of repentance. That is, true confession is not only admitting we have sinned but also that we are willing to change our attitude and actions.

Third, the Bible's prayers of confession recognize that because of our sin we do not deserve to stand before God and ask for His forgiveness. Prayers of confession cannot demand forgiveness because of who we are or what we have done. But with prayers for forgiveness we can be confident that God will forgive because of who God is.

✳ Psalm 32 and 130— Personal Prayers for Forgiveness

Psalm 32 is one of the seven penitential psalms (along with Psalm 6, 38, 51, 102, 130, and 143). These seven psalms are examples of how to pray to God when we recognize that we have sinned. Since ancient times the Christian church has used these psalms on special days set aside for us to confess our sin and admit to God that we have not lived according to His Law. The church recognized that the proper way to deal with guilt is confession.

Blessed is the one whose transgression is
     forgiven,
  whose sin is covered.
Blessed is the man against whom the Lord
     counts no iniquity,
  and in whose spirit there is no deceit.
For when I kept silent, my bones wasted away
     through my groaning all day long.
For day and night Your hand was heavy
     upon me;
  my strength was dried up as by the heat
     of summer.
                              Selah

I acknowledged my sin to You,
> and I did not cover my iniquity;

I said, "I will confess my transgressions
> > to the LORD,"

> and You forgave the iniquity of my sin.
> > > *Selah*

Therefore let everyone who is godly
> offer prayer to You at a time when You may
> > be found;

surely in the rush of great waters,
> they shall not reach him.

You are a hiding place for me;
> You preserve me from trouble;
> You surround me with shouts of deliverance.
> > > *Selah*

I will instruct you and teach you in the way
> > you should go;

> I will counsel you with my eye upon you.

Be not like a horse or a mule, without
> > understanding,

> which must be curbed with bit and bridle,
> or it will not stay near you.

Many are the sorrows of the wicked,
> but steadfast love surrounds the one

who trusts in the LORD.

Be glad in the LORD, and rejoice, O righteous,

and shout for joy, all you upright in heart!

Psalm 32 is a typical psalm of confession. The psalmist begins by reminding himself of the blessings of forgiveness and pardon. The Lord no longer accuses those whom He has forgiven, and those people have stopped deceiving themselves about their sinful actions. That blessing is what drew the psalmist to prayer. He may have felt uncomfortable in confessing his sins. He may have felt that he would lose face in front of others by admitting he was wrong. But the psalmist valued God's forgiveness and the blessings it brings more than he feared the consequences of admitting his sin.

The psalmist had already experienced the consequences of hiding his sin. It affected him not only spiritually and emotionally but also physically. He groaned, felt his guilt in his bones, and lost his strength. Many physicians and psychologists recognize that physical ailments can have spiritual and psychological causes. The psalmist knew that long ago. Other psalms speak of physical burdens caused by sin.

O LORD, rebuke me not in Your anger,

nor discipline me in Your wrath.

Be gracious to me, O LORD, for I am

languishing;

heal me, O LORD, for my bones are troubled.

My soul also is greatly troubled.

(Psalm 6:1–3a)

For my iniquities have gone over my head;

like a heavy burden, they are too heavy

for me.

My wounds stink and fester

because of my foolishness,

I am utterly bowed down and prostrate;

all the day I go about mourning.

For my sides are filled with burning,

and there is no soundness in my flesh.

I am feeble and crushed;

I groan because of the tumult of my heart.

O Lord, all my longing is before You;

my sighing is not hidden from You.

My heart throbs; my strength fails me,

and the light of my eyes—it also

has gone from me.

(Psalm 38:4–10)

Guilt showed itself through psychological and physical ailments in the lives of these psalmists. They had tried to cope with their guilt, but its effects on their lives made it unbearable. What really motivated them to admit their wrongs and pray for forgiveness was not the negative consequences of their feelings of guilt, but the positive blessings promised by God. Those blessings are what the psalmist first mentioned in his prayer, and they were the focus of his plea to God.

Thus the first lesson we learn from Psalm 32 is important. *Prayers of confession should neither be prayed as an easy way out* of our guilt nor as a way to escape the negative consequences of sin. Prayers of confession should be prayed because we trust God's promise of forgiveness. For the psalmist, confessing his sin was not merely saying he had sinned. It was not a quick and easy way to escape his sin. It was not a psychological game to clear his conscience. Rather, it was a prayer of trust in God.

The psalmist acknowledged that God answered his prayer. "I acknowledged my sin to You, and I did not cover my iniquity; I said, 'I will confess my transgressions to the LORD,' and You forgave the iniquity of my sin" (Psalm 32:5). The psalmist does not tell us exactly how he received God's forgiveness. Perhaps, in keeping with Old Testament practices, he went to the temple, confessed his sins, offered a sacrifice, and received forgiveness through the priest. But whatever way he received forgiveness from God, it changed his life.

First, the psalmist's attitude toward God changed. He developed a closer relationship with his Lord. He called God his hiding place and looked to God for protection. The psalmist found comfort in knowing that God surrounded him with the joy that comes in knowing that God had saved him from his sin and guilt. That joy freed the psalmist from the need to sin. We often sin because we aren't comfortable with God's ways of doing things. We do not trust that God is completely in control of everything in life, so we attempt to do things our way. We take shortcuts around God's Law and try to make our lives better because of our selfish, self-centered impulses. We may sin because we try to gain something for ourselves or avoid losing something that we have. We do not trust that God will provide all that we need if we follow His way of doing things. The psalmist's life changed because he was now willing to trust God instead of his own self-centered impulse.

In many cases, parents try to counter God's way of accomplishing things in their children's lives. As parents, we want the best for our children. We want to spare them the pain that comes from failure. Parents who automatically blame teachers when their children are having problems in school can actually be working against God's will. If the problem is the student's, the best thing that can be done is to help the child face the problem and learn to rise above it. But instead of allowing God to work through failure and being an aid to a son or daughter's growth, some parents allow their children to escape the challenge to learn by blaming the teacher or the school. Every teacher has witnessed this tragedy of parents who try to spare their children from failure, only to make matters worse. But they also know that parents who accept the challenges God puts before their children help them learn from the challenges, work with God, and accept His will, making it as positive in their lives as it was in the psalmist's life.

The second way the psalmist's life changed was in his attitude toward receiving guidance from God. The psalmist now recognized that instead of organizing his life according to his desires, he could learn from God. When he sinned, he was being stubborn like a mule that needs to have a bit and bridle to guide it. Now that the psalmist had received forgiveness, he was willing to learn from God and ordered his life according to God's instruction, trusting that God would watch over him.

Third, the psalmist now wanted to tell others of the benefits of trusting God. He didn't keep the relationship he had with God a secret, but wanted others to enjoy that relationship. Therefore, the end of his prayer does not speak to God, but to others. It shows us the benefits of trusting in God and receiving His mercy. It urges us to offer prayers of confession.

Recently, I have had the privilege of serving a congregation as interim pastor while they search for a new pastor.
In this congregation there is a remarkable phenomenon.
Although I can serve only part-time and am not able to do all
the things that a full-time, permanent pastor would do, the
congregation continues to add new members. The reason for
this is not because I am leading an evangelism effort for the
congregation (which I don't have the time to do). Instead, it
is because members of the congregation tell others what they
know about the Gospel of Jesus Christ and what it does in their
lives. They have experienced the change in their relationship
with God because they have received forgiveness from Him.
That forgiveness brings comfort and peace to their lives when
they are assured God is no longer angry with them for their
sins. They know that the forgiveness they need is given at
the Lord's Supper, where Jesus comes in His body and blood.
Often the people of God confess their sins and their pastor
forgives them. They participate in the joy of salvation, the
very presence and mercy of God at His holy altar. Therefore,
they naturally share that joy with others and this brings new
members to the church. These Christians have found what the
psalmist found, and they tell others about it.

These changes in the psalmist's life that we find in his
prayer lead to a second conclusion about prayers of confession: *True prayers of confession are also prayers of repentance.*
That is, true confession is not only admitting we have sinned
but also it is a willingness to change our attitude and actions.
The psalmist did not believe in a cheap confession that admitted his wrongdoing but then did nothing about it. He believed
that true confession involved a willingness to change his life.
This willingness came from the forgiveness and mercy he
received from God. Because of the psalmist's new relation-

ship with God based on God's mercy, he wanted to change. Receiving true forgiveness from God brought him into a relationship that he wanted to have with his Lord permanently. This meant that the psalmist wanted to change his attitude toward God's Law and his behavior toward others. Recognizing sin is the first step in going to God in prayer and confessing our sin. But other steps are involved in prayers that confess our sins. The outcome of all those steps is a changed attitude that is the result of our new relationship with God.

Notice that the same concerns are found in another prayer of confession in the Bible, Psalm 130.

Out of the depths I cry to You, O Lord!
O Lord, hear my voice!
Let Your ears be attentive
to the voice of my pleas for mercy!
If You, O Lord, should mark iniquities,
O Lord, who could stand?
But with You there is forgiveness,
that You may be feared.
I wait for the Lord, my soul waits,
and in His word I hope;
my soul waits for the Lord
more than watchmen for the morning,
more than watchmen for the morning.
O Israel, hope in the Lord!
For with the Lord there is steadfast love,

and with Him is plentiful redemption.

And He will redeem Israel

from all his iniquities.

This psalm shows the same concerns as Psalm 32. It is a confession of sin based on God's mercy, and it shows the psalmist's changed attitude as a result of God's mercy. Yet this psalm highlights another basic truth about biblical prayers of confession. The psalmist asks the rhetorical question, "O Lord, who would be able to stand if You kept a record of sins?" The answer to this question is "No one." As the next line in the prayer states, it is only God's forgiveness that allows us to continue living. This psalm teaches us another truth about prayers of confession: *Because of our sin, we do not deserve to stand before God and ask for His forgiveness.* The Bible's prayers of confession recognize that because of our faults and errors we do not deserve God's forgiveness. Prayers of confession cannot demand forgiveness because of who we are or what we have done. But prayers for forgiveness can be confident that God will forgive because of who God is. It was God Himself, Jesus Christ, who suffered the wrath of God for our sins. Because of Jesus' work of salvation, God has unlimited forgiveness, as the psalmist tells us. Prayers of confession, like all other prayers, focus on the work of Christ, not on the person who is praying.

☀ Ezra's Group Prayer for Forgiveness

The Bible also contains prayers of confession prayed by groups. When Ezra was informed that his people had disobeyed God's Law, he prayed in front of God's temple where he was joined by many others (Ezra 10:1). His prayer is recorded in Ezra 9:6–15:

> O my God, I am ashamed and blush to lift my face to You, my God, for our iniquities have risen higher than our heads, and our guilt has mounted up to the heavens. From the days of our fathers to this day we have been in great guilt. And for our iniquities we, our kings, and our priests have been given into the hand of the kings of the lands, to the sword, to captivity, to plundering, and to utter shame, as it is today. But now for a brief moment favor has been shown by the LORD our God, to leave us a remnant and to give us a secure hold in His holy place, that our God may brighten our eyes and grant us a little reviving in our slavery. For we are slaves. Yet our God has not forsaken us in our slavery, but has extended to us His steadfast love before the kings of Persia, to grant us some reviving to set up the house of our God, to repair its ruins, and to give us protection in Judea and Jerusalem.
>
> And now, O our God, what shall we say after this? For we have forsaken Your commandments, which You commanded by Your servants the prophets, saying, "The land that you are entering, to take possession of it, is a land impure with the impurity of the peoples of the lands, with their abominations that have filled it from end to end with their uncleanness. Therefore do not give your daughters to their sons, neither take their daughters for your sons, and never seek their peace or prosperity, that you may be strong and eat the good of the land and leave it for an inheritance to your children forever." And after all that has come upon us for

our evil deeds and for our great guilt, seeing that You, our God, have punished us less than our iniquities deserved and have given us such a remnant as this, shall we break Your commandments again and intermarry with the people who practice these abominations? Would You not be angry with us until You consumed us, so that there should be no remnant, nor any to escape? O Lord the God of Israel, You are just, for we are left a remnant that has escaped, as it is today. Behold, we are before You in our guilt, for none can stand before You because of this.

Ezra's prayer began as personal, prayed in a public place. It soon became a public prayer. Ezra's confession is an interesting one. He notes, "From the days of our fathers to this day we have been in great guilt." He confesses that not only he and his people in his day had sinned but also his ancestors had sinned. Is Ezra claiming that he is guilty because of the sins of his ancestors? No, rather, he notes that one of the sins he and his people have is that they did not learn from the sins of their ancestors. God punished the kings and priests that went before them for not obeying His commands. Now they had also disobeyed God's commands to them.

Moreover, the sins of Ezra and his people were worse. God gave them new opportunities. They were permitted to return to the land their ancestors lost. However, they repeated the sins that cost their ancestors the land. But despite all of that, Ezra prayed and confessed the sins of his people. Although he did not directly ask for God's forgiveness, his prayer clearly relies on God's promise to forgive those who confess their sin, even though they had repeatedly ignored God's command to them.

One interesting aspect of this prayer is that the sin confessed is one that Ezra was not personally guilty of committing. His prayer revolves around one command that God gave to His ancient people—not to intermarry with the idolatrous people of Canaan (see Exodus 34:12–16). Ezra had not done this, but he confesses this sin because a number of his people had. Perhaps he assumed that he was partially responsible because he had not spoken out against the marriages in time to prevent the people from entering into marriages that God had forbidden. However, even if that was not Ezra's motivation, he recognized he was part of a society that was ignoring God's commands, and he needed to confess the sins of his people, including himself.

We can use this as a guide for prayers of confession today. Many Christians decry the evils that they see in society. Christians even seek to use political means to change laws that they understand to be immoral. None of that is wrong in itself, but how often do we pray to God about the sins of our society and plead for forgiveness? Even if we have not taken part in the particular immoral or unethical aspects of our society, shouldn't we, like Ezra, confess those sins?

We need to confess the sins of our society because we are part of society. No matter which society we as Christians are a part of, we are affected by it. The solutions to our society's problems are not solved by us self-righteously viewing ourselves completely separate from our culture and unaffected by its sins. If Ezra had done that, he would have created a distance between himself and the people who were disobeying God's command. By remaining a part of a society that was ignoring God's command, he was able to pray a prayer that transformed his society. His prayer was a request for forgiveness that would touch the lives of every one of his people so they all would change.

We ought to pray prayers of confession about our society's ills, including confessing our role in the evils that afflict our society and its people. Christians are always a part of society. At times we take part in the practices and assumptions that are common to our culture, not realizing that they may be at odds with God's will. Prayers of corporate confession prayed publicly in church or privately at home are a beginning in the fight to overcome the ills of our culture.

※ Daniel's Private Prayer for Mercy Toward an Entire People

The Bible records two private prayers of corporate confession. The one we will examine in Daniel 9:4–19 tells us:

> I prayed to the LORD my God and made confession, saying, "O Lord, the great and awesome God, who keeps covenant and steadfast love with those who love Him and keep His commandments, we have sinned and done wrong and acted wickedly and rebelled, turning aside from Your commandments and rules. We have not listened to Your servants the prophets, who spoke in Your name to our kings, our princes, and our fathers, and to all the people of the land. To You, O Lord, belongs righteousness, but to us open shame, as at this day, to the men of Judah, to the inhabitants of Jerusalem, and to all Israel, those who are near and those who are far away, in all the lands to which You have driven them, because of the treachery that they have committed against You. To us, O Lord, belongs

open shame, to our kings, to our princes, and to our fathers, because we have sinned against You. To the Lord our God belong mercy and forgiveness, for we have rebelled against Him and have not obeyed the voice of the LORD our God by walking in His laws, which He set before us by His servants the prophets. All Israel has transgressed Your law and turned aside, refusing to obey Your voice. And the curse and oath that are written in the Law of Moses the servant of God have been poured out upon us, because we have sinned against Him. He has confirmed His words, which He spoke against us and against our rulers who ruled us, by bringing upon us a great calamity. For under the whole heaven there has not been done anything like what has been done against Jerusalem. As it is written in the Law of Moses, all this calamity has come upon us; yet we have not entreated the favor of the LORD our God, turning from our iniquities and gaining insight by Your truth. Therefore the LORD has kept ready the calamity and has brought it upon us, for the LORD our God is righteous in all the works that He has done, and we have not obeyed His voice. And now, O Lord our God, who brought Your people out of the land of Egypt with a mighty hand, and have made a name for Yourself, as at this day, we have sinned, we have done wickedly.

O Lord, according to all Your righteous acts, let Your anger and Your wrath turn away from Your city Jerusalem, Your holy hill, because for our sins, and for the iniquitites of our fathers, Jerusalem and Your people have become a byword among all who are around us. Now therefore, O our God, listen to the prayer of Your servant and to his pleas for mercy, and for

Your own sake, O Lord, make Your face to shine
upon Your sanctuary, which is desolate. O my
God, incline Your ear and hear. Open Your
eyes and see our desolations, and the city that
is called by Your name. For we do not present
our pleas before You because of our righteousness, but because of Your great mercy. O Lord,
hear; O Lord, forgive. O Lord, pay attention and
act. Delay not, for Your own sake, O my God,
because Your city and Your people are called by
Your name.

In the first part of this prayer of confession, Daniel contrasts God's faithfulness to His promises with the unfaithful-
ness of Daniel's people. God's great act of faithfulness that
Daniel mentions is that God shows mercy to those who love
and obey Him. Daniel admits that even those who obey God
must rely on His mercy. Even if we obeyed God perfectly (and
none of us have) we still would have to rely on God's mercy.
Our Creator does not owe us anything. Yet He is merciful. He
promised to show mercy to those who loved Him and obeyed
Him (Exodus 20:6), and He went beyond that promise. Israel
not only disobeyed God but also rebelled against Him. In His
mercy God sent prophets to warn His people about the consequences of their rebellion and to invite them to keep His Law
again. They refused, which Daniel admits in his prayer.

The second part of his prayer contrasts God's compassion and forgiveness to the people's rejection of that forgiveness. Note that in Daniel's prayer, acknowledgment of God's
forgiveness is lived out by obeying God. The person who has
truly received God's forgiveness *wants* to live the way God
teaches us to live. However, Daniel had to admit that they
"have not obeyed the voice of the LORD our God by walking in

His laws, which He set before us by His servants the prophets. All Israel has transgressed Your law and turned aside, refusing to obey Your voice" (Daniel 9:10–11a). The word translated *law* is the Hebrew word *torah*.

However, the *torah* denotes more than the idea of laws that tell us what to do or what not to do. It is more than a way for people to rigidly determine what they should do in every situation by applying a set of laws. The root meaning of *torah* is "instruction." God instructed His people in how they were to live. They received laws in the context of instructions to show one another love, mercy, and forgiveness—the things that God showed them. When God's people did not show these things toward others, they showed that they had rejected God's forgiveness. Daniel's prayer admits that Israel received God's punishment because they rejected God's forgiveness.

The third part of Daniel's prayer is a request. He asks God to forgive his people again. He bases his request on God's great act in the Old Testament—leading the people out of Egypt. Throughout the Old Testament, this one great act of God is the defining moment of Israel's relationship with the Lord. When they were totally helpless, with the mightiest army in the world bearing down on them, God parted the Red Sea and saved them. They did nothing and God did everything (Exodus 14:13–14). By picking this example Daniel is again relying on God to do everything needed to grant his request.

The final section of Daniel's prayer calls on God to listen and repeats that he is relying on God and His compassion and forgiveness. He admits that the reason that God should act is not because Daniel or his people deserve it, but because God and His deeds deserve to be recognized by all people.

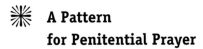 A Pattern for Penitential Prayer

Focus on God

Daniel's prayer combines all the lessons learned about confessing our sins in prayer. His prayer also shows us a way to organize our prayers of confession. A good way to begin a prayer of confession (or any prayer for that matter) is to start with a description of God. Daniel began: "Lord, You are great and deserve respect as the only God. You keep Your promise and show mercy to those who love You and obey Your commandments." Daniel focused his prayer on God by speaking about who God is. In this case, the things he said about God were appropriate to his prayer. They told God why he was praying and helped Daniel to remain focused on the things about God that prompted his prayer.

Pray for Your Need

The next thing that we can mention in our prayer is our need. In this case, Daniel mentioned the need of his people by first noting what they were in contrast to God. They needed forgiveness because they were unlike God. God was faithful; they were not.

Pray about What God Has Already Done for You

After mentioning our need, we can focus on what God has already done for us. In Daniel's day, that was the release from slavery in Egypt. For Christians today, God's defining act is the life, death, and resurrection of Jesus. In Jesus, God has freed us from the slavery to sin and death—precisely what we are praying about in our prayers of confession.

Pray for Forgiveness,
Healing, and Change

Finally, we can bring our request for forgiveness and healing to God. In this request we cannot only ask for forgiveness but also for God to heal us. The result of the healing is that we change our sinful ways. Therefore, the results of forgiveness show in our lives in concrete ways. Depending on what we are confessing, these results may be different things at different times. However, it is an important part of our attitude toward God's forgiveness. Daniel wanted change for his people. He did not state directly what he wanted that change to be. However, by praying that God would lift His anger against Jerusalem, Daniel was implying that his people would be changed so they would return to Jerusalem. There they would worship God and live according to His teachings that He gave through the prophets. We should also want God to change us so His teachings through the prophets and the apostles make a difference in the way we live.

While our prayers of confession do not have to follow this outline, it is a wise and useful one. It can help us focus on God and His mercy and make our prayers ones of true confession and real repentance. It is not easy for us to admit our guilt, even to God. Our pride does not want to admit that we are not worthy of God's mercy and compassion. Moreover, we don't want to rely on God's mercy and forgiveness given to us, even though we have sinned. Admitting that draws an even sharper contrast between God and us. We do not measure up in that contrast. Yet the only way to really deal with our sins in a healthy way is to learn to pray prayers of confession such as the ones we have looked at in this chapter. God forgives our sins and mends our lives that have been broken by our own failures. When we learn that, we learn to pray and confess. Often the result is that we will find it impossible to delay our prayer.

Nehemiah 1:5–10 is the second prayer of confession. It is a prayer by Nehemiah about his people's sins and his desire to help them as they rebuild Jerusalem. In a sense it is a follow-up to Daniel's prayer. You may also want to look at a few psalms of confession, especially Psalm 15, 52, and 79 as well as three of the seven penitential psalms not treated in this chapter: 51, 102, and 143.

4

When Health Fails

Health and fitness have become an obsession for many in the United States. News programs on radio and television regularly feature items on health, fitness, and medicine. Many newspapers even have weekly sections devoted to health issues. We receive constant advice on diet, exercise, and ways to prevent disease. We hear of new medical procedures and treatments, and we are aware of how much our medical knowledge has increased our expected life spans.

However, none of this knowledge seems to have stopped us from worrying about our health. No matter how good our medical knowledge has become, we are still subject to infirmities caused by the spread of disease, our environment, and the inevitable process of aging. Knowing more about the causes of disease as well as prevention and treatment has not meant that we are immune from the threat of disease. We can spend thousands of dollars or even an entire life's savings on treating ill health, but we cannot escape disease, sickness, or death.

It is not as if we don't try to escape ill health. Access to health care has become an important issue for public policy in the United States. Those who do not have health insurance desperately want it, or they want access to treatment through a government program. Those who do have health insurance are at times reluctant to leave one job for another because they are afraid their new company's health insurance may not cover them or their family. Systems of national health insurance have been proposed, but they have not been adopted because of fears that a new system will be too expensive or the care will not be as good.

Why all this fear of ill health? Part of our fear is a quality of life issue. We know that chronic ill health can mean our lives are complicated by physical limitations, pain, and loss of income. Another part of our anxiety is fear of death. Ill health can be a prelude to death. In fact, for most of human history, when people were so sick that they could not get out of bed, people assumed death was near. We seldom speak of someone being on his or her deathbed today, but the fear of sickness leading to death remains.

However, there is a reason that our society has such an obsession with avoiding ill health. Spiritual poverty leads us to desperation when we face our mortality. We often cling to physical health so tightly because we have a real lack of spiritual health. In our contemporary worldview we have frequently divorced our physical and spiritual lives from each other. Instead of using a time of sickness or ill health as a reflection on our well-being from all perspectives, we repeatedly moan and complain about our physical state and neglect our spiritual side. Some are so spiritually impoverished that when a loved one is near death they will urge physicians to do every possible treatment. They do this even though the physicians may have advised them that little or no hope exists for successful treatment. Instead of turning to spiritual resources, we are tempted to turn to highly advanced medical procedures or even experimental and nonconventional treatments to save us.

What do the prayers in the Bible teach us about dealing with failing health? Can we find in the prayers of the Scriptures a way to achieve a proper balance between physical and spiritual needs in times of sickness? We can find this balance when we learn two important lessons that the prayers we will examine teach us: (1) *Trust in God leads to prayers that are able to bring all of our concerns, pains, frustrations, and worries openly to God.* (2) *Our God is greater than everything in this life. He will outlast our life and our world.* During poor or failing health we can praise God because we know He will have compassion on us no matter what the outcome of our disease.

☀ Hezekiah's Prayer for Healing

A variety of approaches to the problems of failing health are evident in biblical prayers. King Hezekiah presented one approach when he was told by the prophet Isaiah that he was dying. He prayed simply: "Now, O LORD, please remember how I have walked before You in faithfulness and with a whole heart, and have done what is good in Your sight" (2 Kings 20:3).

In this short prayer Hezekiah pointed out he had not only done what God considered the right thing to do but he had also done it sincerely. Hezekiah reformed Israel's worship and campaigned to rid Israel of idolatry. He was faithful to the Lord in the face of the most powerful army of his day—the Assyrians. All of this was unusual for the kings of Judah. Very few of the kings had been as faithful to the Lord as Hezekiah had been. His zeal for God is told to us not only in the Book of Kings but is also noted in Isaiah and hinted at in Proverbs (see Proverbs 25:1). Hezekiah appeals to this love for the Lord in his prayer.

However, Hezekiah's prayer does not infer that God owes him a favor because of the faithfulness he had shown throughout his life. He begins his prayer with *please*. This word occurs only 13 times in the Hebrew Bible. *Please* is a special word for a sincere request—never a demand or expectation. Hezekiah recognized that God did not have to allow him to live. His faith was not going to fail if God allowed him to die. Yet Hezekiah does remind God of his exemplary life and asks God to take that into account.

In Hezekiah's case, God heard his prayer and granted his request. Hezekiah lived for fifteen more years. God granted Hezekiah, one of the most faithful kings of Judah, longer life. Isaiah records for us Hezekiah's prayer of thanks to God for the gift of health and a longer life (Isaiah 38:9–20).

But that is not all we learn about Hezekiah's reaction to God's gift. Unfortunately, Hezekiah did not use his gift of health properly. In 2 Kings 20:12–19, Isaiah 39:1–8, and 2 Chronicles we read about Hezekiah's foolish pride when ambassadors from Babylon came to visit him.

> But Hezekiah did not make return according to the benefit done to him, for his heart was proud. Therefore wrath came upon him and Judah and Jerusalem. But Hezekiah humbled himself for the pride of his heart, both he and the inhabitants of Jerusalem, so that the wrath of the LORD did not come upon them in the days of Hezekiah. (2 Chronicles 32:25–26)

Here we learn two things about God's answer to Hezekiah's prayer. First, we see that God's original intention that Hezekiah die may have been better, but God nevertheless granted Hezekiah's request. Second, we learn that Hezekiah allowed God's answer to prayer to become a temptation. He became conceited, and this self-centered attitude led him to neglect his devotion to God. But Hezekiah remained a man of God despite his conceit. When he recognized his sin, he and his people confessed. Instead of remaining conceited, they learned once again that humans cannot claim any special status before God because of who they are or what they have done.

We can learn some valuable lessons from Hezekiah's prayer, God's response, and how Hezekiah reacted. First, we can learn that while human physical frailties are difficult for us to accept when they strike us, they can be what is best for us. While we pray to be released from the effects of sickness or injury, God may know that we can serve Him better or be better off with our limitations. Hezekiah became conceited when he was allowed by God to overcome the physical limitations of death. We also can be tempted to think too highly of ourselves when we enjoy good health that allows us to live without the humbling effect that sickness or injury might bring. This same lesson was taught to the apostle Paul when he prayed to God and asked for improved health. God reminded Paul that his physical weakness allowed Paul to trust God's strength (2 Corinthians 12:7–10).

Many people today are obsessed with maintaining not only good health but also youthfulness. We want to reverse the effects of aging because it brings on physical limitations. Most 40-year-old people cannot do everything they did at 20, because our bodies slow down. We have small aches and pains. At 50 or 60 or 70 we cannot expect to be as physically active as we were when we were younger. Countless products are sold with the appeal that they will make us appear younger or feel younger. We spend money on exercise machines in a vain attempt to remain youthful. If the intent is to stay as physically fit as God will allow us, exercise and fitness are good things. Is our pursuit of youthfulness an unspoken prayer to God to reverse what He has determined to be best for us? Are we ignoring the blessings that can come with age? Perhaps our aging is a chance for a more mature appreciation for His gifts and a slower physical pace that allows us to contemplate all that He does for us.

Death is the result of sin, but it can be a blessing for believers. It is a release from the pains of this life so we can be with our God. For unbelievers, death can never be a blessing—only a transition into eternal death. Yet death may also be a way for God to keep us from sins that would embitter our lives or the lives of others, had we lived longer.

Like Hezekiah, we may pray for health and life. God may grant us our prayer's request. When He does, we need to use God's answer as an opportunity to appreciate our health as a gift from God that we do not deserve. God gives us that gift to use humbly in His service.

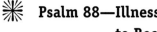 Psalm 88—Illness as an Opportunity to Become Closer to God

When we are sick, our main concern is not serving, but being served. We can see that in several of the prayers about sickness in the Bible. One of them is Psalm 88:

When Health Fails

O LORD, God of my salvation;
    I cry out day and night before You.
Let my prayer come before You;
    incline Your ear to my cry!
For my soul is full of troubles,
    and my life draws near to Sheol.
I am counted among those who go down
        to the pit;
    I am a man who has no strength,
like one set loose among the dead,
    like the slain that lie in the grave,
like those whom You remember no more,
    for they are cut off from Your hand.
You have put me in the depths of the pit,
    in the regions dark and deep.
Your wrath lies heavy upon me,
    and You overwhelm me with all Your waves.
                   Selah

You have caused my companions to shun me;
    You have made me a horror to them.
I am shut in so that I cannot escape;
    my eye grows dim through sorrow.
Every day I call upon You, O LORD;
    I spread out my hands to You.

Do You work wonders for the dead?
  Do the departed rise up to praise You?
                    Selah

Is Your steadfast love declared in the grave,
  or Your faithfulness in Abaddon?
Are Your wonders known in the darkness,
  or Your righteousness in the land of
    forgetfulness?
But I, O Lord, cry to You;
  in the morning my prayer comes before You.
O Lord, why do You cast my soul away?
  Why do You hide Your face from me?
Afflicted and close to death from my youth up,
  I suffer Your terrors; I am helpless.
Your wrath has swept over me;
  Your dreadful assaults destroy me.
They surround me like a flood all day long;
  they close in on me together.
You have caused my beloved and my friend
    to shun me;
  my companions have become darkness.

The writer of this psalm had such a severe illness that he began to think about his death. His physical illness became a spiritual struggle. As the psalmist felt himself come closer to death, concerns about his spiritual well-being and his relationship with God became as important as his physical concerns. He speaks about being as good as dead, coming closer to the grave and going "down to the pit." (*The pit* is a frequent term in the Old Testament for the place where the dead go.) But notice what the psalmist then says:

> I am a man who has no strength,
>
> like one set loose among the dead,
>
> like the slain that lie in the grave,
>
> like those whom You remember no more,
>
> for they are cut off from Your hand. (4b–5)

At first, the psalmist appears to be talking about what his extreme illness has done to his relationships with other humans. He is as good as dead and, therefore, abandoned by others and placed in a grave. However, his concern remains with his relationship with God. The psalmist worries about what death will bring to his spiritual life. Will he be cut off from God? Will he die spiritually as well as physically? What will happen to him eternally when death comes?

That, after all, is the real concern that we have about death. Will death be the end of everything for us? If it is not, will death bring us something better? Many people, perhaps even most people in Western societies, live as if nothing follows when this life ends. That is why we want all the things we can get in this life. Polls taken in recent years in the United States show that most people believe God exists. However, behavior of people in our society shows we do not live as if our belief in God means anything practical after death. We tend to believe that this life is what counts. We want to feel younger, have more possessions and wealth, and enjoy pleasures of all sorts. Pornography, drugs, moral relativism, and violence pervade our society. One of the reasons for this is the lack of our trust that God can provide for us something other than this life. The most valued ideal for many people in society has become enjoyment of life. That may mean engaging in whatever makes us as individuals happy, feel better, or helps us avoid physical, mental, and spiritual pain.

The psalmist was in the midst of that pain. Moreover, he attributed some of that pain to what God had done. He said to God, "Your wrath lies heavy upon me," then went on to list the things God had done to bring him pain. God pounded at him with waves of misfortune. God took his friends away and made him disgusting to them. God locked him in his circumstances with no escape. Later, the psalmist talked about suffering since he was young and always near death. He complained that God's anger was upon him and he had been destroyed by terror from God. The psalmist raised the question of whether God would provide for him after death. Would his sickness lead to death, then nothing? Will he lose the only thing that could possibly endure beyond the grave—his relationship with God?

What we read in Psalm 88 is a cry for a relationship with God that not only transcends the grave but also addresses the problems of ill health that the psalmist had. The two cannot be separated. As we become ill or develop a chronic disease, we cannot separate our present problems from our eternal future.

Is it all right for us to call on God to address our sickness and disease while expressing our concern about whether He will provide for us beyond this life? Is the psalmist's prayer a prayer that expresses an unhealthy doubt about God's power? Is it an affront to God and an insult to His divine power? We could understand it that way, but I would suggest that we would be misreading his prayer.

This prayer is a healthy airing of the psalmist's concerns. His experience could only tell him about this life. As a human being, he could only imagine what life beyond this world must be like. He could not see it, experience it, or even speak to those who are now enjoying it. If the psalmist's faith in the promise of God to provide a better life beyond the grave wavered, the healthy thing to do was to raise his concerns and make them part of his prayer. It was better than engaging in behavior that seeks to deny death or numb the pain of life and the effects of ill health. The psalmist could have lashed out at his friends. He could have despaired of having any hope and sought to numb his pain with alcohol. Instead, he took his physical, psychological, and spiritual pains to God through his prayer.

Psalm 88 may seem to be a list of doubts and complaints that ends in despair. However, it is a healthy, spiritual cry for God's help in restoring the psalmist's physical, mental, and spiritual health. He openly lays out his concerns. That could only happen as a result of his trust in God.

When we have a chronic disease, or even when we are dying, we need to learn to pray as the psalmist did. In other words, we need to learn: *Trust in God leads to prayers that are able to bring all of our concerns, pains, frustrations, and worries openly to God.* That is what the writer of Psalm 88 did. We do not know what answer he received to his prayer. But his prayer was preserved for us in the Bible so that we might learn to openly and frankly bring all of our concerns to God, especially when our health fails. The psalmist probably gave us his prayer to show us that true spiritual health trusts God enough to boldly pray about concerns, knowing God will listen. Today, we believers know that because of Jesus Christ and His work,

God opens His ears to us. In forgiveness and grace, we can approach the compassionate throne of God with all of our concerns. The psalmist is a great example of this. He shows us that God would rather hear our doubts and conflicts than allow our ill health to become a time of losing our spiritual well-being.

※ Psalm 102—Illness as an Occasion to Praise God

In Psalm 102 we find another prayer of a person whose health failed. He prayed:

Hear my prayer, O LORD;

let my cry come to You!

Do not hide Your face from me

in the day of my distress!

Incline Your ear to me;

answer me speedily in the day when I call!

For my days pass away like smoke,

and my bones burn like a furnace.

My heart is struck down like grass and has

withered;

I forget to eat my bread.

Because of my loud groaning

my bones cling to my flesh.

I am like a desert owl of the wilderness,

like an owl of the waste places;

I lie awake;
    I am like a lonely sparrow on the housetop.
All the day my enemies taunt me;
    those who deride me use my name for
        a curse.
For I eat ashes like bread
    and mingle tears with my drink,
because of Your indignation and anger;
    for You have taken me up and thrown
        me down.
My days are like an evening shadow;
    I wither away like grass.
But You, O Lord, are enthroned forever;
    You are remembered throughout all
        generations.
You will arise and have pity on Zion;
    it is the time to favor her;
    the appointed time has come.
For Your servants hold her stones dear
    and have pity on her dust.
Nations will fear the name of the Lord,
    and all the kings of the earth will fear
        Your glory.
For the Lord builds up Zion;
    He appears in His glory;

He regards the prayer of the destitute

    and does not despise their prayer.

Let this be recorded for a generation to come,

    so that a people yet to be created may praise

        the Lord:

that He looked down from His holy height;

    from heaven the Lord looked at the earth,

to hear the groans of the prisoners,

    to set free those who were doomed to die,

that they may declare in Zion the name

        of the Lord,

    and in Jerusalem His praise,

when peoples gather together,

    and kingdoms, to worship the Lord.

He has broken my strength in midcourse;

    He has shortened my days.

"O my God," I say, "take me not away

    in the midst of my days—

You whose years endure

    throughout all generations!"

Of old You laid the foundation of the earth,

    and the heavens are the work of Your hands.

They will perish, but You will remain;

    they will all wear out like a garment.

You will change them like a robe, and they will
　　pass away,
　　but You are the same, and Your years have
　　　　no end.
The children of Your servants shall dwell secure;
　　their offspring shall be established
　　　　before You.

In this prayer the psalmist begins with his call to God. He begs God to listen and to respond quickly. The reason for this urgency is his failing health. The psalmist describes his illness as having two effects: It is eating away at his lifetime and his body.

As the psalmist's ill health continues, he speaks of his days disappearing like smoke. It is as if his days vanish into thin air. They are gone and can never be recovered. Later, he speaks of his days as being like a shadow that is growing longer. The setting sun at the end of a day causes shadows to become longer and longer. The psalmist's illness has brought him to the twilight of his life, with the long shadows telling him that his days of life are few.

The psalmist's illness not only eats away his days but also his body. The psalmist is so ill that he cannot eat. He has lost so much weight that he is skin and bones. And because he cannot eat, he knows that his spirit is broken: "My heart is struck down like grass and has withered." His illness and broken spirit combine to deprive him of sleep, furthering his illness.

These things in themselves would make anyone miserable enough to cry out in prayer for deliverance from sickness, but another thing added to the psalmist's misery. His enemies used his sickness as a way to insult him. They used his name as a curse! They gloated over his illness and seemed to have been saying he deserved his poor health.

Often, when someone suffers a tragedy, some people will react by blaming the person who is suffering. It can even become an excuse for not showing mercy and kindness. "He brought it on himself. He'll have to live with the consequences," can be an excuse to do nothing to help someone in pain. When a smoker suffers from lung cancer or emphysema, it is easy to blame the victim. We can be less than sympathetic and have an excuse for not being as supportive as we ought to be. Some people shun those who have AIDS. Because this disease is often transmitted by homosexual behavior, it is easy to bring a moral judgment against AIDS victims, even those who contracted the disease in another way. Some AIDS victims have had to endure not only the shame that many associate with the disease but also unwarranted discrimination in public services and employment. The psalmist's enemies were using his illness in that way, and even going further to find satisfaction for themselves in his illness.

The psalmist's frustration with his illness and the gloating of his enemies led him to his real complaint. He told God: "For I eat ashes like bread and mingle tears with my drink, because of *Your* indignation and anger; for *You* have taken me up and thrown me down" (Psalm 102:9–10, *my emphasis*). The psalmist's concern over his health was coupled with his concern that God had vented His anger on him and then abandoned him. In his failing health and approaching death, he needed to know that even though God had allowed him to suffer, God would not be forever hostile toward him.

Suddenly, the prayer shifts its tone. The psalmist remembers that God is eternal, that God never ceases to be God. Because God is always God, His nature never changes. He is a

God of mercy, and the psalmist begins to praise God for His mercy. He remembers that God will have mercy on Zion, that God builds Zion, and is praised in Zion. Of course, the application is not merely to the mountain on which Jerusalem was situated. Zion was the city where God's people worshiped and prayed to Him. The psalmist pictures God's mercy to all of His people and proclaims: "He regards the prayer of the destitute and does not despise their prayer" (v. 17). His prayer then turns into praise for God, who hears the groans of prisoners and rescues people condemned to death. The psalmist may have felt like a prisoner to his disease, but he now could rejoice because he knew that God would not abandon him forever.

Where can we find Zion for us? Just as God always located Himself to show mercy to His people in the Old Testament, God also locates Himself today. God comes to us in His Word and in the sacraments He gives to the church. In other words, we have access to God and His mercy when we read His Word or go to church. Church is today's Zion, a place where God gives His word, mercy, and forgiveness to His faithful people. It is for this reason that so many ill people need their pastor or another believer to bring God's Word to them. Sometimes it is in the home, at other times it is in the hospital or a nursing home. People need God and His Word the most when they are sick, especially when it appears that sickness will soon bring death.

Would the psalmist be cured and go on living? His prayer does not tell us. In fact, in the last section of this psalm he restates that he has been weakened and his life has been shortened. Yet in his prayer he found comfort in the God who never dies, who will exist even when all of creation ceases to exist. The psalmist may die, but God will continue to be merciful to him and those who come after him. The psalmist ceased to be concerned about whether he would be cured. His prayer led him to the confidence that God was greater than his illness, that God was greater than anything he could have in this world—even if he lived to be cured. He still prayed that God would not allow him to die in the prime of his life, but he was content to know that God would never cease being merciful.

The prayer we know as Psalm 102 leads us to another lesson about prayers we might pray during sickness or ill health. *God Himself, Jesus Christ, overcame sin, the devil, and even death. Our God is greater than everything in this life. He will outlast our life and our world. During poor or failing health we can praise God because we know He will have compassion on us no matter what the outcome of our disease.*

☀ Jesus Shows Us How to Pray When Our Life Is Ending

Perhaps the ultimate outcome of failing health is death. It is one thing to pray when we are so sick that we feel as if we are dying. It is another thing to pray when we know that we are dying. What can we pray for then? Of course, we may want to pray for others—our family, our friends—and ask God to watch over them. We may also wish to pray that God would forgive those who mistreated us during our lives. However, what are we to pray about for ourselves? Jesus' example shows us how we are to pray when dying. His short prayer on the cross as He died demonstrates how we should pray: "Then Jesus, calling out with a loud voice, said, 'Father, into Your hands I commit My spirit!' And having said this He breathed His last" (Luke 23:46).

Jesus had many concerns as He was dying. He was concerned about His mother, and He provided for her (John

19:26). He was concerned about those who persecuted and executed Him, and He prayed that they might be forgiven (Luke 23:34). Jesus even took time to have compassion on one of the other men who was crucified with Him (Luke 23:43). However, His final thoughts when dying turned to God. Jesus placed Himself into His Father's hands. At the point of death we have no one and nothing else to turn toward. We can only trust in the work of God Himself, or despair of having anything beyond the grave. Jesus trusted in the will of God the Father. He shows us that in all of life, and especially in death, our only hope is to trust in God's will. It was the Father's will that Jesus live a holy life in our place. It was the Father's will that Jesus pay for the sins of the whole world and suffer for those sins on the cross. It was the Father's will that Jesus willingly give up His spirit and die for us. It was the Father's will that Jesus conquer death and rise on the third day. When health fails for the last time, no amount of medical technology that can prolong our lives is able to match the loving arms of a Father in heaven who is willing to receive us as His dear children into life with Him.

Jesus' prayer has taught other Christians how to pray when their health is failing. We see it again in Scripture when Stephen was dying. "And as they were stoning Stephen, he called out, 'Lord Jesus, receive my spirit' " (Acts 7:59). He placed his spirit in the hands of Jesus, who had placed His spirit into the hands of the Father.

But how can we prepare ourselves to face our own death when it comes? We will die but once, so we can't rely on experience. Where will we find the strength to pray like Jesus or Stephen when we are dying? God gives us many chances throughout our lives to practice for the final failure of our health. We can start with church, where we first died and rose with Christ in our Baptism, as St. Paul teaches us (Romans

6:1–6). When we witness Baptisms in church, we learn to pray based upon the promises of forgiveness, faith, the Holy Spirit, and the new life that our Baptism gives to us. We can learn to pray when we attend the Lord's Supper where we sing God's praises with angels and archangels and all of the company of heaven. There, we are praying with the saints who have died in the faith. God created all of life, and in the forgiveness of sins we know that we live forever with Him. There we actually participate in a foretaste of the resurrected life, the feast to come.

We can use our times of illness as times of prayer and reflection. Our illness only shows us our frailty in this sinful world. By faith, we know the resurrected body is ours. We know, by faith in Jesus, we are holy, spotless, and without blemish. This is a time of tremendous contrast between the sinful world and the sinless world, which is ours by faith but will soon be ours in all reality. We can pray for God to focus our lives on Him and His promises so we can be better prepared for the time when we will die.

We can reflect on the end of life whenever a relative, friend, or acquaintance dies. If the person was not Christian, it only intensifies our zeal for the proclamation of the Gospel of Jesus. If that person was a Christian, we can pray that God would help us learn from their example of faith to help guide us when we face death. We can use their funeral as a time to contemplate the things God's Word says about Baptism, death, and eternal life and pray about them. We can learn from these experiences to place all of life in God's hands so when death comes, we are prepared to pray as Jesus and Stephen did. Their prayers were based upon the will of the Father and the promises of the Gospel. We, too, can confidently pray and submit our spirit to the heavenly Father, who looks upon us as dear children in the light of Christ.

When our health fails for the last time, or when we are with someone else who is dying, a short prayer placing our spirits in the hands of Jesus and His Father is enough. The ultimate answer to prayer when health fails is God's will and the promises it offers in Jesus.

⊱─◈─O─◈─⊰

The psalms contain many prayers that mention sickness as one of their concerns (see Psalm 38, 39, and 69). I would recommend a study of this topic in the psalms as a way of learning more about praying during illness.

5

When Family Provides Support

What is the most significant relationship in adulthood? Some would argue that it is their relationship with their occupation. Much of our adult existence revolves around our job, and we often relate to other people on the basis of what we do. Yet our occupation does not span or define our entire adulthood. We spend our adolescence and early adulthood in education, defining and preparing for our future career. In our current economy, many people change employers, jobs, and even careers several times. In April 1993, *The Economist* reported that only 25 percent of U.S. workers could expect to stay in their present job twenty years or more. That same month *Money* magazine reported that the average job tenure in corporate United States has shrunk to less than seven years. In addition, those who live to retirement age often live a significant portion of their adult life without an occupation.

Those who have children often feel that the most significant relationship of adulthood is parenthood. In one sense, they are right. Parents are second in authority on this earth only to God. Martin Luther writes: "[God] distinguishes father and mother above all other persons on earth, and places them next to Himself."[1] Parents' lives seem to revolve around their children, feeding them and changing diapers when they are young and guiding them through childhood to adolescence to adulthood. Parenting—if done conscientiously—takes time, effort, and dedication. It often brings us friends who have children the same age as our own as we participate in school, civic, or church activities for the benefit of our children. All families flow from parents. This seems to be an obvious statement, but with that reality comes the authority and honor of parents. Yet children grow up and become adults. We may remain their parents, but we are no longer parenting them. Parenthood, though an important part of many adult lives, is not the defining relationship of adulthood.

However, there is one set of relationships that is significant for the vast majority of adults—family relationships. Moreover, the relationship that has been the center of family life throughout human history is marriage. Even those who never get married are affected by marriage. Most likely their parents were married. If their parents were not married, the lack of that relationship can have profound effects on their childhood, as the current concern over single-parent families demonstrates. Therefore, we should also seek to learn what the Bible tells us in its prayers concerning family and marriage.

The Bible recognizes the benefits of marriage and presents it as the norm for most adults. The Old and New Testaments both speak of marriage as God's gift for the benefit of humans. With all of this support for marriage and recognition of its benefits, surprisingly few of the prayers of the Bible speak about marriage. In addition, few are about the blessings of marriage and family. We will examine the few that do exist: Hannah's prayers in 1 Samuel 1:10–13 and 2:1–10 (both set in the context of a spouse who was supportive) and Psalm 128 and 133, which speak of that support coming not only from a spouse but also from other members of a family. As we examine these prayers, we will discover another principle about prayer: *God is not only the origin of prayer but He also supports us so we can pray.* In the prayers we look at in this chapter we will see how God uses spouse and family as part of that support.

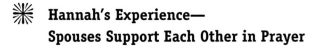

Hannah's Experience— Spouses Support Each Other in Prayer

Hannah's prayers never mention her husband or her family, even though these form the basis of the two prayers in 1 Samuel. Hannah's first prayer grew out of trouble in her family and the expectations of society. She was one of Elkanah's two wives. Like many women in the ancient Near East, Hannah tried to live up to the common expectations of wives in her day—to produce children for her husband. However, Hannah had no children. Elkanah's other wife, Peninnah, had several sons and daughters. Although Hannah was unable to have children, the Bible offers us evidence that Elkanah was still devoted to her. When he sacrificed to the Lord at Shiloh, we read that he not only gave portions of the sacrifice to Peninnah and her children but that he also gave a portion to Hannah. The Bible tells us that Elkanah did this even though the Lord had kept Hannah from having children (1 Samuel 1:5). Elkanah did not allow his love for her to depend on what she could do, but he loved and supported her even when she could not do what was expected of a "good wife."

Peninnah especially tormented Hannah over her lack of children when Elkanah took them to worship at the Lord's house. Perhaps we know what Peninnah was saying. The Lord blesses husbands and wives with children (Psalm 127:3–5; see also Genesis 29:31). Peninnah might have been telling Hannah that the Lord was withholding His blessing from her. So the time spent in sacrifice and worship at Shiloh was a time of misery for Hannah. She felt separated from God and perhaps even from her husband, even though he supported her. When Hannah cried and refused to eat, we can almost hear the disappointment and frustration in Elkanah's voice when he said to her: "Hannah, why do you weep? And why do you not eat? And why is your heart sad? Am I not more to you than ten sons?" (1 Samuel 1:8). Elkanah supported Hannah, but she remained downhearted because she could not live up to society's expectations of her.

Despite all of this, Hannah still went to God in prayer. She prayed for a son and promised God: "O Lord of hosts, if You will indeed look on the affliction of Your servant and remember me and not forget Your servant, but will give to Your servant a son, then I will give him to the Lord all the days of his life, and no razor shall touch his head" (1 Samuel 1:11). Hannah made a type of vow to the Lord that is explained in Numbers 6. The person who takes this vow is called a Nazirite. Nazirites were forbidden to drink alcohol or vinegar, drink anything made from grapes, or eat grapes or raisins. They also were forbidden to cut their hair. In the Bible we know of only three Nazirites, all of whom were placed under this oath from birth. Two of them would serve as judges of Israel— Samuel and Samson. The third, John the Baptizer, is the only Nazirite mentioned in the New Testament (see Luke 1:15). The Nazirite was especially dedicated to the Lord. Hannah was showing her devotion to the Lord in her prayer by promising she would raise her son to be loyal to Him. Hannah's vow is remarkable because she was willing to dedicate the son she wanted so dearly to the Lord. Keeping her vow meant that at a very young age her son would leave her. Yet she was willing to return the Lord's gift to Him.

However, Hannah wasn't the only one willing to make this sacrifice. Numbers 30:1–14 informs us that husbands had the right to cancel the vows their wives made to God. Elkanah never canceled his wife's vow. He supported her even though it required him to give up his son. Elkanah, despite his disappointment and frustration with his wife's depression over not bearing children, sympathized with her. He knew her pain and was willing to sacrifice so that she could keep her vow. Hannah prayed with confidence because of the support of her husband.

When we think of the benefits of marriage, we might consider many of the blessings of love, support, and comfort that spouses can offer each other. However, we seldom consider how marriage can be a blessing in our praying to God. People, such as Hannah, who have the support of their spouses can rely on that support in prayer. If our spouses support us, we can pray about our wants and needs with the confidence that our spouses will be part of God's plan to supply all that we need. A supportive, godly husband or wife provides added strength to a spouse's prayer. The blessings of being married to a partner who is not only loving but who also loves God translates into spiritual support as we bring our requests to God.

However, the story of Hannah's prayer does not end with her request for a son. After God answered her prayer and provided a son, she returned to God's house to dedicate her son. There she prayed again:

My heart exults in the Lord;

    my strength is exalted in the Lord.

My mouth derides my enemies,

    because I rejoice in Your salvation.

There is none holy like the Lord;

    there is none besides You;

    there is no rock like our God.

Talk no more so very proudly,

    let not arrogance come from your mouth;

for the Lord is a God of knowledge,

    and by Him actions are weighed.

The bows of the mighty are broken,

    but the feeble bind on strength.

Those who were full have hired themselves out

        for bread,

    but those who were hungry have ceased

        to hunger.

The barren has borne seven,

    but she who has many children is forlorn.

The Lord kills and brings to life;

    He brings down to Sheol and raises up.

The Lord makes poor and makes rich;

    He brings low and He exalts.

He raises up the poor from the dust;

    He lifts the needy from the ash heap

to make them sit with princes

and inherit a seat of honor.

For the pillars of the earth are the Lord's,

and on them He has set the world.

He will guard the feet of His faithful ones,

but the wicked shall be cut off in darkness,

for not by might shall a man prevail.

The adversaries of the Lord shall be broken

to pieces;

against them He will thunder in heaven.

The Lord will judge the ends of the earth;

He will give strength to His king

and exalt the power of His anointed.

(1 Samuel 2:1–10)

This prayer shows us a Hannah in the opposite frame of mind from her first prayer. She prayed her first prayer while she was depressed. It was a short, one sentence prayer of 26 words (in Hebrew). Hannah was so upset and downhearted she could hardly find the words to pray. In contrast, Hannah prayed this second prayer when she was joyful.

Hannah's joy is evident from the beginning. She prays about the joy the Lord has given her and acknowledges that He alone could give her such joy. "There is none holy like the Lord . . . there is no rock like our God." That is what we would expect from a person of faith, but in the middle of the first part of Hannah's prayer we find a disturbing thought: "My mouth derides my enemies." Hannah expresses some contempt for those who made her feel miserable when she was unable to bear children. (That could have included Peninnah, but may also have included others in society who looked down on her when she was childless.) Is she taking the vindication God gave her and turning it into selfish joy and delight? Or is this attitude something that is proper? The answer to these questions comes in her next thought. "I rejoice *in Your salvation*." Hannah's mocking is connected with God's actions.

The prayer goes on to explain why she mocked others. Hannah reminds everyone who speaks arrogantly that the Lord is in charge of all things. The middle of her prayer speaks of the power of God to change the fortunes of humans. He is in control of human strength, life and death, honor and shame. God can transform human situations so those who are lowly or needy become honored. He can also make those who are powerful weak. God can even give childless women children. Hannah is mocking the arrogance of those who place their trust in human abilities and worldly power and status. That is what Peninnah did. She used her blessing in this world as if they were her own instead of God's. Hannah acknowledged that her son was God's and was willing to dedicate him to God.

Hannah's enemies arrogantly thought that humans controlled their fate. They took advantage of their blessings from God to bring misery on Hannah instead of giving thanks to God and offering comfort and support to her. However, Hannah knew that humans could not succeed by their own strength. She mocked those who thought that they could use their strength without God's blessing and in ways He never intended. Her mocking was a reflection of God's attitude toward such arrogance.

The arrogance that Hannah felt bearing down on her when she could not have children was not merely the torture of having to endure the taunts of Peninnah. Peninnah was merely reinforcing what society already was communicating—that women who could not have children were less than adequate as wives. In our day, society has different values about marriage and family. Some of them are in keeping with God's will, but others are not.

For instance, some parents feel inadequate if they cannot provide their children with many luxuries. However, good parenting is more than merely providing the latest toy or game for our children. Supportive spouses who know this do not make each other feel guilty that they cannot give their children things. Good parents give their children the emotional and spiritual gifts that modern Western society often overlooks. When spouses support each other, they are led to prayer and find what Hannah found there—a God who supports them through their spouses. They find a God who "lifts the needy from the ash heap to make them sit with princes and inherit a seat of honor" (1 Samuel 2:8).

In examining the circumstances of Hannah's prayer we have discovered another principle about prayer. In chapter one we discovered that prayer originates with God. Now we learn that *God is not only the origin of prayer but He also supports us so that we can pray.* That support can come in many ways. In this chapter we see that God supports us through family, especially through spouses. However, this does not mean that those who are not married have less support from God than those who are. Other family members can offer the support we need. Even those Christians who do not have any living family members receive support through their family in Christ—their brothers and sisters in the faith.

Such support is important, even when we are separated from those who provide our support. Although Hannah was not physically separated from her husband, she felt isolated from him when she could not bear any children. Yet his support helped her pray. Christians who are physically separated from their loved ones often draw on the knowledge that others support them as they pray. Christians have been imprisoned for their faith and have been separated from their loved ones by war or natural disasters. But they have still found strength in knowing that God has others in this world who love them and are concerned for them. We can even find examples of this in the Bible. For instance, when Paul was in prison he wrote to the Philippians:

> I thank my God in all my remembrance of you, always in every prayer of mine for you all making my prayer with joy, because of your partnership in the gospel from the first day until now. And I am sure of this, that He who began a good work in you will bring it to completion at the day of Jesus Christ. It is right for me to feel this way about you all, because I hold you in my heart, for you are all partakers with me of grace, both in my imprisonment and in the defense and confirmation of the gospel. For God is my witness, how I yearn for you all with the affection of Christ Jesus. (1:3–8)

Just as Paul felt the support of his brothers and sisters in Christ as he prayed in prison, we also are supported by God through those whom He has placed around us. Those who have a Christian spouse find that support as part of the special relationship of marriage that God has given to humans.

※ Family Members Support One Another in Prayer

When we look at the Book of Psalms, we find two prayers that tell us about the importance of support from spouse and family. One of these is Psalm 128.

> Blessed is everyone who fears the LORD,
>> who walks in His ways!
>
> You shall eat the fruit of the labor of
>>> your hands;
>>
>> you shall be blessed, and it shall be well
>>> with you.
>
> Your wife will be like a fruitful vine
>> within your house;
>
> your children will be like olive shoots
>> around your table.
>
> Behold, thus shall the man be blessed
>> who fears the LORD.
>
> The LORD bless you from Zion!
>> May you see the prosperity of Jerusalem
>> all the days of your life!
>
> May you see your children's children!
>> Peace be upon Israel!

This psalm is a prayer for blessings for the person who is faithful to God. It asks blessings of prosperity for everyone who not only believes God's promises but who also strives to live as God wants them to live. This psalm asks six blessings for such a person: food provided by labor, a wife who prospers, children who provide blessings, prosperity from Jerusalem, grandchildren, and peace for Israel. Of these six blessings, three come through family: wife, children, and grandchildren. Of those three, wife is listed first. While children and extended family members are important, the value of a good spouse outweighs them all, and the psalmist shows us this by mentioning wife before other family members.

The sequence of blessings in this psalm is deliberately planned. The psalmist begins by mentioning the blessing of receiving a good reward for labor. This first blessing is one that would enable a person to contribute to a family's well-being. By being able to earn enough so that he could feed himself (and perhaps feed others as well) the recipient of this blessing would be a blessing to others. He could have a wife and children.

The next blessing is a spouse—and specifically a wife because the psalm is addressed to a man. The wife is compared to a fruitful vine. The picture of a grapevine filled with grapes, a major crop, was a common one in ancient Israel. As we do today, ancient Israelites used grapes as fruit and to produce raisins and wine. As we read this psalm we might immediately think that the comparison of the wife to a fruitful vine speaks of the wife bearing children. While this would be a part of the intended comparison, we should not conclude that it is the sole sense in which the comparison is to be understood. The blessing that a wife brings represents not only children but also all the other physical and spiritual blessings that a wife can provide for her husband. This is borne out by the other blessings mentioned in this psalm: children and grandchildren are mentioned, but so are prosperity from Jerusalem and peace in Israel. These blessings are primarily spiritual and are part of the blessings wished upon the person addressed in this psalm.

The psalmist's view of a good spouse is not one-dimensional. The husband's contribution is more than support for the family through his labor. The wife's contribution is more than the children she is able to bear. Both contribute to spiritual blessings. The psalmist pictures the wife bearing fruit for the entire household. The blessings that husband and wife give each other include emotional and spiritual blessings for their household. Together they pass those blessings on to their children.

The third blessing, children, follows from the second blessing. The wife not only brings children into the world but also, with her husband, provides a household where those children can grow, learn, and mature physically, emotionally, intellectually, and spiritually. By picturing the children as young olive trees, the psalmist helps us to anticipate the growth of the children, who are ready to shoot up like young, vigorous olive shoots.

Olive trees were prized for their fruit, which provided an important source of dietary fat for ancient Israelites. Because meat was expensive, not always available, and often reserved for special occasions, olives and olive oil were essential foods. Olive oil was an important ingredient in many foods and also served as cooking oil. It allowed average Israelites, who would not otherwise have enough fat in their diet, to remain healthy. The image of children as olive trees pointed toward prosperity and further blessings as the children grew.

Thus, as they grow, the children are pictured as being blessed by their parents and as blessings to their parents. Of course, this presupposes a household where the parent's faith in God's work and blessings guides their lives. The psalmist is assuming that the parents provide for their children's religious training in the Word of God. That is why the next blessing he prays for is the Lord's blessing from Zion, the site of the temple. This family provides support for one another because of the faith that mother and father share with their children. It leads them to focus on God, worship Him, and lift up their prayers to Him.

Such faithful people looked for Jerusalem to prosper. Prosperity was not measured with economic factors: profits by Jerusalem's merchants, riches for its residents, a growing economy, and an ever-shrinking lower class. Rather, prosperity for Jerusalem was the result of the prosperous work of God on earth. In other words, God faithfully kept the children of Israel in His mercy and care. God showed His people how much He loved them and forgave them through the many ceremonies and actions associated with the temple and daily life. God was active in the way He saved and preserved Israel—all for the sake of the messianic promises and their salvation. This meant that people honored God as they worshiped Him in the temple, as sacrifices were brought to Him, and as prayers were made to Him. Throughout the prophecies of the Old Testament, and especially in the accounts recorded in the Books of Kings and Chronicles, prosperity for Jerusalem was tied to the temple of God and worship there, where God made His presence known. When the family received God's blessings, they were also receiving them as the community of the children of Israel. Therefore, the blessing of the family that faithfully worshiped together benefited all of God's people. In turn, a spiritually healthy community was a blessing to that faithful family. The psalmist wishes this blessing to last all the days of the life of the person who reads this psalm.

Then the psalmist moves on to another blessing, grand-children. Here he adds a third generation who can benefit from the blessings that began with the husband and wife. Of course, this blessing implies a long life. However, it also implies that all the blessings of this psalm will endure so the grand-parents can rejoice that God gives the same blessings to their grandchildren as He had given to them.

Living long enough to see one's grandchildren may not be perceived as a blessing if those grandchildren are born into a world without hope of prosperity. For the faithful follower of God, living to see one's grandchildren is a blessing if those grandchildren are taught the fear and honor of the Lord that their grandparents have. The implication of this blessing is that the faithful parents had a strong marriage in which the hus-band and wife supported each other in their life and their faith as they both grew spiritually. Those parents hand their values and faith down to their children who, in turn, hand it on to the grandchildren. The psalmist is wishing a blessing of long life for his readers and also wishing them a lifelong blessing. He wishes his readers a strong and enduring marriage character-ized by both partners' strong and enduring faith in God.

This leads to the final line and blessing of the psalm: "Peace be upon Israel!" Peace among God's people is impor-tant. When God's people are beset with arguments and strife, maintaining one's faith becomes difficult. It also becomes difficult for families to worship together with God's people if the church has constant bickering and quarrels among its members. Sometimes families have withdrawn from attending weekly worship services because their congregation had inter-nal clashes. In contrast, the psalmist wishes peace for Israel—

God's people (see Galatians 6:16). When such peace exists, all the other blessings of this psalm are enhanced.

However, the Hebrew word *shalom*, which is translated *peace*, means more than an absence of hostilities. It also contains the idea of the presence of good and proper relationships among people. That is what the psalmist wants God's people to enjoy. They do not merely cover over their antagonistic feelings, grudges, and prejudices toward one another by making an outward peace that belies inward hostilities. They also live together in true inward peace because they have forgiven one another as God has forgiven them. This type of peace supports Christian families, and those who have such peace support other Christians. Therefore, this psalm that began as a prayer for blessings upon individuals and their families ends as a prayer for the entire family of God.

Viewing God's people as a family is an important metaphor used throughout the Bible. It is also an important theme in the last prayer about family life we will examine, Psalm 133.

> Behold, how good and pleasant it is
>> when brothers dwell in unity!
> It is like the precious oil on the head,
>> running down on the beard,
> on the beard of Aaron,
>> running down on the collar of his robes!
> It is like the dew of Hermon,
>> which falls on the mountains of Zion!
> For there the Lord has commanded the blessing,
>> life forevermore.

This psalm speaks of the blessings when family members live together. The Hebrew word translated *brothers* can mean family members in general and is used of nephews (Genesis 14:14, 16), cousins (1 Chronicles 23:22), and other close relatives. It can even refer to female relatives (Deuteronomy 15:12; 2 Chronicles 28:8). In this psalm it may have an even wider meaning. We might refer to someone who has a close common bond with us as a brother or sister, even though they are not related to us in any way. Similarly, this psalm may be speaking of those who share the common bond of faith in God as brothers and sisters. Paul used the same language in his letter. This psalm may be using the term *brothers* in the wider sense to denote those who are not siblings. However, we can understand it only if we first understand its implications for actual family members—real brothers and sisters. Then we can begin to understand its extended meaning.

Of course, brothers and sisters do not always live in harmony. Sibling quarrels are a part of this life. They may be conflicts over petty jealousies and feelings that parents often have to deal with. Or they may be fights over inheritances that can divide brother from brother and sister from sister. However, the psalmist pictures the blessings that come when brothers and sisters are able to live in harmony and put aside their bickering. He compares such harmony with fine, scented oil poured on the head of Aaron, Israel's first chief priest.

The image of oil poured on a head is not a pleasant one for us, but it was for the Israelites. Olive oil had many uses for the ancient Israelites. It served as food as well as fuel for lamps. Perfumed and scented olive oil was a cosmetic applied to hair and skin to make them appear healthy and smell pleasant. Often hosts at a party would anoint their guests in a sign of goodwill and favor toward them (see Psalm 23:5). In addition, olive oil was part of special ceremonies to induct people into high offices. In these ceremonies oil was poured on the person's head. This anointing symbolized God's pouring His Holy Spirit out upon the person. Thus we can read about Saul and David being anointed as kings (1 Samuel 10:1; 16:13). In Leviticus 8:12 we read about Moses anointing Aaron to be chief priest of Israel. It is this anointing to which Psalm 133 refers.

The psalmist uses the picture of anointing in an interesting way. He begins by saying that the harmony between brothers and sisters is like oil on the head. Perhaps the first thought is that the psalmist is referring to the use of oil to beautify and perfume the hair. Then the psalmist extends the picture to oil running down on the beard. We might now be led to think of anointing someone for an office. On the other hand, we might still think that this is speaking of perfuming one's head of hair and perhaps also the beard, as at a party. Then the psalmist adds that the oil is running down Aaron's beard and onto his robes. Now we are given the picture of God pouring out His Spirit on Aaron as he becomes high priest.

In his skill as a poet, the psalmist has combined a number of pictures to show us how pleasant harmony among family members is. It reminds us of beauty and sweet perfume. More than that, it reminds us of God's blessing on us when He sends us His Holy Spirit to give us faith and guide us in life. Our anointing into the family of God took place at our Baptism. What a beautiful understanding of the gift of the Holy Spirit. When we were anointed by the Holy Spirit in Baptism, we were given our callings as children of God. In our baptismal anointing God made us members of the children of Israel. Zion is our home, our resting place, our comfort. This is where we find peace in the midst of our troubled world. This piling up of pictures powerfully communicates what harmony among family members is. It is something we can appreciate and enjoy as we might enjoy beauty and sweet smells. However, we can enjoy it because it comes from God as He pours out His Holy Spirit on us. True family harmony is a gift from God.

Then suddenly, the psalmist switches images and speaks of family harmony as dew on Mount Hermon, the highest mountain in the Anti-Lebanon mountain range. It marked the northern limits of Joshua's conquests (Joshua 11:17; 12:1). Because snow covers Mount Hermon year-round, it serves as a major source of water for the Jordan River. Throughout most of the year the evaporation of water from the snow of its peaks allows dew to form on its slopes. In contrast, the land around Mount Hermon is arid. In a land where rainfall is critical and water shortages can lead to death of crops, cattle, and people, dew is critically important for life. The picture is of an area where life can flourish.

As the psalmist started with one picture of anointing and moved to another, here also he transforms the picture of life-giving dew. The dew falls on the mountains around God's holy mountain, Zion. They, like Mount Hermon, enjoy dew. Because Mount Zion was the location of God's temple, the flourishing life is now transformed from the physical life of plants and animals to spiritual life that only God can give. In fact, the psalmist makes this clear. Zion is where God promised the blessing of eternal life.

We now have a complete picture of the harmony that the psalmist is speaking about—one shared by those who have eternal life through faith in Jesus Christ. The family harmony that God wishes us to have is not just a pleasant home life, but a harmony that comes from sharing the promise of eternal life. Peace in the home comes through forgiveness as the family learns to forgive each other as Jesus forgives them. The support that husbands and wives can give to each other is founded on the eternal life they share in Christ. The harmony of brothers and sisters who have been taught the promises of God in Jesus and share the faith of their parents is more than the love that non-Christians have for their siblings. It is a love deepened and enhanced because brothers and sisters share the love of God that comes only through forgiveness of sins. This harmony is then extended to our brothers and sisters in Christ. Because we share one heavenly Father, we can live in peace and harmony with one another. How good and pleasant that is!

We started this chapter with a story about disunity and discord in a family. As we consider the Bible's various prayers, we can see that God wants us to have unity, harmony, and peace in our families. However, the only lasting harmony we can have in our families comes from God Himself. It begins when husband and wife share not only their common bond of marriage but also the bond of unity in Christ Jesus. Unity in Christ is enjoyed only where there is forgiveness of sins. We are one with God only because of the blood of the one holy sacrifice of Jesus. That sacrifice on the cross brought forgiveness to the world. That blood of Jesus cleanses us and makes us holy to stand in God's temple where He dwells. When spouses support each other in life and in prayer, the height of their unity is in the forgiveness they share with each other. They accept each other as holy, forgiven children of God. That brings peace and unity to their marriage. In turn, they pass that same forgiveness and support down through their generations so the true peace that only God can establish becomes a part of family life.

6

When Prayer Becomes True Prayer

How should we pray? Christians have always sought ways to pray and have wanted to learn how to pray properly. The questions that I have been asked about prayer in my duties as a pastor and professor usually had to do with the *content* of prayer. I was often asked, "Are certain requests appropriate in prayer?" I have never encountered someone who wanted to ask for something in prayer that they thought was directly against God's will. For instance, I have never been asked whether a request that is clearly against the explicit meaning of the Ten Commandments was appropriate for a prayer. Instead, the request usually questioned whether a certain heartfelt desire was appropriate, or whether it was selfish and therefore against the spirit of God's Law.

These questions about whether we should include certain requests in our prayers are not always easily answered. We have already examined biblical prayers in which the requests for punishment of enemies were a central concern. In the last chapter we examined Hannah's prayer for a child, which certainly was a prayer that included one of her most personal desires. Praying for a heartfelt, personal need is not necessarily wrong. How can we pray for those needs and at the same time not fall into the sin of placing our personal desires above God's will? To answer this question we need to examine some of the Bible's prayers that can serve as models and patterns for our prayers. We will also learn two more important principles about prayer: *God's Word, the Scriptures, is the foundation upon which prayers are built. We need to center our prayers on God's promises.*

In addition, the Bible's prayers will teach us how to construct our prayers. One question I have never been asked about prayer, but one I suspect lies behind many of the requests, involves the mechanics of composing a prayer. How should I word my prayers? What should I put first? We know to start a prayer with some reference to God and to close it with *Amen.* However, many Christians feel that they do not quite know how to arrange the thoughts and requests they want to include in their prayers. Often they are reluctant to lead others in prayer. After all, their prayers do not sound like the well-organized prayers during worship services. By examining prayers in the Bible we can learn about the patterns used in biblical prayers and how to compose our own prayers (even as we are praying them).

❋ Learning from Jesus What to Ask for in Our Prayers

Of course, the most familiar prayer intended to serve as a model of Christian prayer is the Lord's Prayer. It is found in two places in the Bible with different forms. In Matthew it is part of the Sermon on the Mount (Matthew 5–7). In Luke we are told that it is Jesus' instruction to His disciples when they asked Him to teach them how to pray. The form of the prayer in Matthew is the one prayed by Christians as the Lord's Prayer. Luke's version is slightly differently than Matthew's version. Moreover, the version in Luke omits two of the thoughts found in Matthew's version.

Matthew 6:9–13:

Pray then like this:

"Our Father in heaven, hallowed be Your name.

Your kingdom come,

Your will be done, on earth as it is in heaven.

Give us this day our daily bread,

and forgive us our debts, as we also have

forgiven our debtors.

And lead us not into temptation,

but deliver us from evil."

Luke 11:2–4

When you pray, say:

"Father, hallowed be Your name.

Your kingdom come.

Give us each day our daily bread,

and forgive us our sins,

for we ourselves forgive everyone

who is indebted to us.

And lead us not into temptation."

The Opening of the Lord's Prayer— God as Father

Scholars have long recognized that the Lord's Prayer contains seven requests or petitions. (Luke's version contains only five. We will explore possible reasons for the omission of the third and seventh petitions.) Before giving these petitions, Jesus taught His disciples to address God as *Father*. This was the way Jesus addressed His prayers (see Matthew 11:25–26; 26:39 [or its parallels Mark 14:36; Luke 22:42]; 26:42; Luke 10:21; 23:34, 46; John 11:41; 12:27–28; 17:1–25). Throughout the Sermon on the Mount, Jesus referred to God as their Father (Matthew 5:16, 45, 48; 6:1, 4, 6, 8, 14, 15, 18, 26, 32; 7:11, 21). While God was occasionally referred to as a father in the Old Testament (Psalm 103:13; Proverbs 3:12), no prayers address Him as Father. Jesus is the one who teaches us about our relationship with God as our Father. That relationship brings us to God in prayer, trusting that He loves as a perfect Father who listens to His children's requests and who wants to give them every good thing. In other words, praying to God as our Father focuses us on the First Commandment. It reminds us we should have no other gods that we trust (see Exodus 20:3–6).[2] When we pray to God as *our Father*, we are saying that we trust only Him.

The early Christians understood this and prayed to God as their Father. Paul reminded his readers that when they prayed, they called on God using the Aramaic word for father, *Abba* (Romans 8:15; Galatians 4:6), just as Jesus did (Mark 14:36). Of course, we have other ways of addressing God in prayer. However, Jesus and Paul both emphasized that when we pray, we should understand the close relationship that God has with us. When we believe in Christ and all that He has done for us, we become children of God who know His love. This should lead us to pray with the confidence that God wishes to hear our prayers and is always ready to listen to our requests. Moreover, this should make us bold in prayer so that we do not hold back our thoughts and desires from God when we pray. Instead, because we know that our Father loves us, we can bring all our thoughts and requests to Him.

However, Jesus instructs us to pray this prayer together. Individual Christians are not to think of themselves as if they were God's only child and pray "*My* Father." Instead, Christians are to pray together and for the common good. Therefore, Jesus taught His disciples to pray "*Our* Father." While Luke's form of the prayer begins simply "Father," it also assumes Christians are praying for their common good. Luke quotes Jesus as saying: "When you [*plural* in Greek] pray . . . " Moreover, both Matthew and Luke tell us that Jesus taught His disciples to pray: "Give *us* . . . ," "Forgive *us* . . . ," "Don't allow *us* . . . " Calling on God as *our* Father does more than remind us of our relationship to one another. If God is our Father, we are brothers and sisters. Jesus instructs us to pray as united family members who have the love of the Father and who love one another.

The address to God also reminds us that He is our Father *in heaven*. Our relationship with Him (and, therefore, with our brothers and sisters) is a spiritual one. Jesus is teaching us to pray to our Father in heaven so we learn that our prayers transcend our earthly limitations. We pray to God in heaven so the earthly barriers of culture, language, social or economic status, race, and age are overcome. Too often we want to identify Christianity with our situation in life. We tend to think of our culture or subculture as somehow embodying Christian characteristics instead of understanding that all human cultures not only contain good but also contain sinful traits and characteristics. In the United States, churches have often been polarized along racial lines. Instead of praying "Our Father" we can be at times praying "My Father (and the Father of those like me)." Yet Jesus reminds us that He came for all people in all races and cultures, of all languages and ages and classes. Earthly divisions are not relevant when we pray to our Father in heaven.

The Organization of the Seven Petitions: Focusing on What Is Important

When we come to our heavenly Father, what should we ask for? As we turn to the seven petitions of the Lord's Prayer, we find that the first three focus on God's work in our lives. The fourth petition focuses on our physical needs, the only petition to speak of any needs for our bodies. The fifth, sixth, and seventh petitions are requests for our spiritual well-being. Jesus is showing us how to construct our prayers so they emphasize our spiritual needs. Because Jesus understood the situation of humans in this world, He knew they tended to be most concerned with their physical needs. He saw this in the many people who followed Him looking for cures for their diseases. Jesus felt the pressure to make Him their king because He could provide them with unlimited food (John 6:15).

We are no different from the people in Jesus' day. Our primary concerns are most often for the physical things we need or think we need. From the air we breathe to the shelter we sleep in and everything in between (food, clothing, possessions), we live in a world where we cannot separate ourselves from the constant physical needs we have. Our physical needs overwhelm us to the point that they often crowd out the most important needs in our life—our spiritual needs. That is why in the Sermon on the Mount Jesus followed this prayer with warnings about concentrating on our physical wants and needs. He warns us about the difficulty of being both rich and a Christian (Matthew 6:19–24) and tells us that life is more than our physical needs (Matthew 6:25–34). In addition, Jesus shows us how to construct our prayers so we do not dwell on our physical needs and neglect our greater spiritual needs. He shows us to begin by asking for things that we know our heavenly Father wants to do for us and to end with requests for spiritual blessings. Jesus does not deny our need for physical blessings, but He shows us that they are nothing without the spiritual blessings from heaven.

The First Petition— Honoring God's Name

What are the things that our heavenly Father wants for us? In the first petition, Jesus teaches us to pray: "Let Your name be kept holy." At first, this may not seem as something our Father wants for us, but for Him. However, God's name is holy by its very nature. What is not holy is our use of it. In this petition Jesus is telling us to pray that we might be given the strength to keep God's name holy. How can we do that?

The obvious way to keep God's name holy is not to use His name in such a way that He is dishonored. We shouldn't speak evil of God or use His name in ways that would bring Him a bad reputation. Among those things are teaching in God's name anything that is not true, anything that is intended to deceive others, or anything that is used to cover up a lie (such as false testimony under an oath sworn in God's name).

However, we are also praying that we do not merely avoid using God's name incorrectly, but that we learn to use it correctly (as in praying to Him). This is an important point, especially for the Jews who first heard Jesus. You see, by Jesus' time, in order to avoid misusing God's name, the Jewish people quit using the name God had used to identify Himself in the Old Testament. God's name, *Yahweh*, ceased to be pronounced by Jews. Instead they substituted the Hebrew word for *Lord*. (That is why in many Bible translations *Yahweh* is translated by LORD [in small capital letters] while the Hebrew word for *Lord* is translated Lord [only the first letter capitalized].) The Jewish people thought that they could avoid misusing God's name if they did not pronounce it. However, God did not give us His name so we would neglect using it out of fear of misusing it. Instead, He wants us to call Him God, Father, and Lord and to teach others to use it correctly.

Speaking God's name is not the only way we can use or misuse His name. The way we live is also included in this petition. We are praying God would teach us to live holy lives so that when others see us they praise the God whom we believe in and serve (Matthew 5:16). When we Christians do not live holy lives but do things that even non-Christians know are wrong, we can cause them to ridicule our God and bring shame on Him and His name.

In the first petition we are asking God to keep His name holy in our lives as well as in our speech. In other words, Jesus is teaching us to pray that God would give us the strength to keep the Second Commandment and honor His name (see Exodus 20:7).

The Second Petition— God's Kingdom among Us

The second petition is a request for God's kingdom to come. In many places, the Bible speaks about the coming of Jesus as king to usher in God's eternal kingdom. Peter urged his readers to look forward to that coming of God's kingdom (2 Peter

3:10–13). Jesus is telling us to pray for that kingdom to come so that it remains our constant hope.

However, God's kingdom also comes in another way. Both John the Baptizer and Jesus told the people of their day that the kingdom of God was near (Matthew 3:2; 4:17). Later, Jesus told the Pharisees that the kingdom of God was among them (Luke 17:21). Paul also told the Colossians that they had been brought into God's kingdom (Colossians 1:13). God's kingdom will come in glory at the end of time, but it also comes to us today in the Good News about Jesus, in Baptism, and in the Lord's Supper. In this prayer we pray that God's kingdom continues to come to others and to us through God's Word. We are asking that God would make us able to hear His promises and believe so we can be members of His kingdom today.

Therefore, this second petition is a prayer that God would help us keep the Third Commandment (Exodus 20:8–11). While that commandment speaks mainly about honoring the Sabbath as a day without work, the Sabbath was never understood as only a day for rest. It was always seen as a day to hear God's Word and be strengthened in faith in God's promises through that Word of God. Jesus endorsed that view of the commandment by preaching in synagogues on the Sabbath (e.g., Luke 4:31).

Jesus did things on the Sabbath that could have been considered work. He cured diseases and approved of other things His disciples did on the Sabbath, such as harvesting wheat for a meal (Matthew 12:1–8). Some thought that Jesus and His disciples were breaking the Sabbath. However, Jesus never spoke against worship on the Sabbath, and He frequently used the Sabbath to bring the good news of God's kingdom to others. He kept the true spirit of the Third Commandment and in reality fulfilled the Old Testament ceremonial laws.

Of course, Jesus does not tell us to pray: "Let Your kingdom come on the Sabbath." He teaches us to pray for God's kingdom to come without any limitation to a particular day. In this prayer Jesus tells us to ask our heavenly Father to send His kingdom constantly. Where there is forgiveness of sins, there is the kingdom of God. Whenever the promises of God's Word are read, heard, or used, this prayer is being answered. This is why the kingdom of God is most obvious in the gathering of His people in church. There, Jesus, the Groom, calls forth His Bride, the church, and He serves us His Everlasting Feast. There one can be confident the kingdom of God is present.

The Third Petition—A Summary of the Introduction and First Two Petitions

The third petition asks that God's will would be done on earth in the same way it is done in heaven. But how is God's will done? An easy and quick answer might be that God's will is done whenever people live according to His Law. Of course, God does want people to live holy lives. However, if we view this request as a prayer that God rigidly enforce His Law, quickly punishing anyone who breaks it, we would be misunderstanding what this petition is asking. God does not desire for people to be forced to live according His Law. He wants them to live according to His Law because they want to live that way. God wants us to do His will out of love for Him as our heavenly Father (the introduction). He wants us to live lives that bring honor to His holy name (the first petition) as grateful members of His kingdom (the second petition). Therefore, in the third petition, when we ask that God's will be done, we are summarizing our prayer to this point. (Perhaps this is why Luke's version does not contain the third petition. Because the third petition summarizes the first two petitions, it can be omitted without changing the meaning or focus of the prayer. Jesus omitted it when He privately taught His disciples how to pray.)

However, we also acknowledge some important truths as we summarize the first part of our prayer. First, we acknowledge that God's name is holy in heaven. That is, those who have gone to heaven before us now live holy lives that honor God's name. As we acknowledge this truth, we look forward to the time when we will join them and be freed from our failures to bring honor to God's holy name.

Second, we acknowledge that God does rule in heaven and that we are looking forward to living in His glorious kingdom with Him as our king. That is, we are longing for the best of all governments—when God rules over us and we can see the full glory of our King. Because of our human failings, we have never lived under a government that is perfect and enjoys the support of all its citizens. However, in this petition we acknowledge that a perfect government does exist and that we are eager to live as its citizens. God has made us members of His kingdom already in this life when He gave us faith in our Savior. We pray in the third petition of the Lord's Prayer that we are longing to live under the full power and glory of that kingdom in the same way as those Christians who are now in heaven.

Therefore, as we close the third petition, we have prayed that God would enable us to keep the first part of His Law—that we love Him with all our heart (Matthew 22:37). In the Ten Commandments, the first three commandments tell us what God expects of those who love Him.

The Fourth Petition—Everything
We Need to Live in This World

The fourth petition of the Lord's Prayer requests daily bread. In one sentence Jesus teaches us to ask for everything we need in life: food, clothing, shelter, possessions, family, friends, health, peace, and any other good thing that is a part of this life. Jesus summarizes all our earthly needs and puts them in the only petition to ask for the non-spiritual concerns of life. While Jesus minimizes the needs that we often feel most, He does not overlook them when He teaches us to pray. As a human being Jesus was acutely aware of our physical, psychological, and social needs. He knew hunger (Matthew 4:2) and thirst (John 19:28). He had family and friends whom He loved (John 19:25–27; John 11:3).

However, Jesus includes those needs in only one petition of the Lord's Prayer. Because we feel the need for these things in this life so acutely, we often make these the major concerns for life and allow them to crowd our spiritual needs out of our thinking. Jesus provides a balance by minimizing our prayers about our daily bread.

Yet when Jesus tells us to pray for these things, He reminds us that our heavenly Father does provide all the needs of life. As we pray for these things, we are praying that God would make us aware that He does provide us everything we need every day. If we know that God provides them for us, we will not have to break any of the last seven commandments, which are concerned with our relationships with other people. They command respect for those in authority (Exodus 20:12), for human life (Exodus 20:13), for marriage (Exodus 20:14), for property (Exodus 20:15), and for others' reputations (Exodus 20:16). They also forbid sinful desires as well as sinful acts (Exodus 20:17). When we realize that God gives us all that we need for our body and life, we do not have any need to break these commandments. In the fourth petition we pray that God would make us thankful for the daily bread that He gives to all people. He even gives it to those people who do not have faith and do not pray for daily bread (Matthew 5:45).

The Fifth Petition—
Acknowledging Our Failures

By the time we come to the fifth petition of the Lord's Prayer, we have already prayed for all our needs according to the Ten Commandments. What is the next thing to pray about? As we pray and ask God to help us to keep His commands, we realize we have not kept them. Every day we stray from His commands. Not everything we do honors God's name. We overlook the many ways in which God gives us our daily bread, and we forget to give thanks for it. Therefore, we need to beg our Father for His forgiveness for our failures. That is exactly what Jesus tells us to do in the fifth petition.

As we pray the Lord's Prayer and meditate on its meaning, we are moved to realize we can receive all these things only if our relationship with our heavenly Father, daily broken by our sin, is daily reestablished. In the fifth petition we ask God to reestablish it. In pleading with Him to forgive us, we acknowledge we cannot restore that relationship. We must rely on Him to keep His promise to forgive us. Jesus tells us to pray for forgiveness so we will never fall into despair and think that God will not forgive us. He teaches us that we can believe God's promise and rely on Him to love His children so much that He is always ready to forgive them.

Moreover, Jesus reminds us that sin not only breaks our relationship with God but also breaks relationships we have with others. Those who sin against us are in need of forgiveness, and Jesus teaches us to forgive others as our Father forgives us. He already taught His disciples that those who show mercy in forgiving others are blessed because they will be shown mercy (Matthew 5:7). Jesus tells us that in our prayers we should promise God to restore the broken relationship we have with others because of their sins against us. He urges us to take the first step in healing wounded relationships in the same way our Father heals our wounded relationship with Him.

The Sixth Petition— Power to Overcome Sin

In the sixth petition, our Lord teaches us to pray that we would not be tempted so that we can avoid sinning. After recognizing our sins, we pray that God would keep out of our lives any temptation that would lead us to sin. However, we are not merely asking God to keep us out of situations where we might feel the urge to sin. We are asking Him to strengthen us so that we can resist temptation.

The Seventh Petition— A Summary of the Fifth and Sixth Petitions

Finally, in the seventh petition, Jesus teaches us to pray that God would keep the evil one, Satan, from gaining control over us through our weaknesses, our desires for things in the world, or through any other of the tools he uses to draw people away from God. Although the Lord's Prayer is traditionally prayed "Deliver us from *evil*," the Greek text of Matthew says, "Rescue us from *the evil one*," using a term for the devil found elsewhere in Matthew (5:31; 13:19, 38). Jesus is teaching us to pray that God would always keep us out of the power of the devil and his temptations. Satan is treated here as the ruler of this world who wants to bring evil into our lives. Therefore,

Jesus wants us to pray that God would guard us from all kinds of evil, especially sin, by keeping us safe from the crafty enemy of our souls.

This last petition of the Lord's Prayer is a summary of the fifth and sixth petitions. In those petitions we pray for forgiveness, promise to forgive others, and pray that we are not tempted to sin. In other words, we are praying that God would keep us from all evils that could plunge us back into spiritual death. We pray for forgiveness so that we do not fall into despair thinking that God has abandoned us because of our failures. We promise to forgive others so we do not deny them the forgiveness that God has given us and turn them away from Christ. Finally, we pray that God would not allow anyone or anything to tempt us. These evils can destroy our souls, and the devil is always trying to use them to separate us from our heavenly Father. Therefore, Jesus adds a summary petition to remind us exactly how seriously they can damage us. Now we can understand why this petition is missing from Luke's version of the Lord's Prayer. Just as Jesus omitted the third petition without changing the thrust or meaning of the prayer, so He omitted the seventh petition without altering its meaning.

Now that we have examined the Lord's Prayer, we can appreciate it as a well-structured and deeply meaningful prayer. Jesus teaches us to pray for the important things in our life by structuring the first part of the prayer (introduction through the fourth petition) on the Ten Commandments. He shows us how to pray for the spiritual power we need so that we can live according to God's will. Then, in the second part of this prayer (the fifth, sixth, and seventh petitions), Jesus teaches us to pray about our failures and our weaknesses. We ask that we will overcome the evil powers of this world that want to prevent us from using the spiritual power that God freely gives His children.

☀ Learning from Jesus to Pray Our Own Prayers

The masterful construction of the Lord's Prayer is part of its power that has moved Christians throughout the centuries to adopt it as a prayer for use in public worship and private devotions. However, Jesus did not teach His disciples this prayer only for repeating word-for-word. He wants us not only to pray the Lord's Prayer but also to learn from it so that we can grow in composing our own prayers.

Can we learn to construct our prayers in the same way? I believe we can. In fact, for hundreds of years the Christian church has used a similar construction in its prayers. In many churches a prayer known as a *collect* (pronounced *có-lect*) is said each Sunday before the reading of the Scriptures. These prayers are designed to focus the worshipers who are gathered together (Latin *collectus*, "gathered") on the theme of the Scripture readings for that day. Most collects follow a simple, but powerful, pattern:

1. The invocation (an address to God)
2. A description of God or of one of His acts that reflects the content of the prayer
3. The petition (a request)
4. The benefit hoped for as a result of the granting of the request
5. A closing, often mentioning the Trinity (Father, Son, and Holy Spirit)

(Not all collects contain all five of these features.)

As we look at prayers in the Bible, we find that many of them contain the first three elements of the collect. The Lord's Prayer follows that pattern: the invocation ("Our Father), description ("who is in heaven"), and seven petitions. In addition, though Jesus did not include a closing for the prayer, the Lord's Prayer is often concluded with: "for thine is the kingdom and the power and the glory forever and ever."[3] Jesus not only taught His disciples a prayer, He gave them a pattern to follow when praying. The church has used that pattern throughout its history. It is an easy pattern to use so we can focus our thoughts on our prayer and not be distracted by things around us. If we learn to pray in this way, we can grow in constructing even our most impromptu, spontaneous prayers so they focus our thoughts clearly and effectively on our concerns, needs, and desires.

For instance, if we wanted to pray for children to be brought to faith in the Savior, we could compose a prayer using the collect pattern or the pattern we find in the Lord's Prayer. Our prayer might be:

Lord Jesus (*introduction*), You taught Your disciples not to prevent little children from coming to You, but to bring them to Your loving arms (*description*). We ask that You would call all children to faith (*petition*) so that they would know the joys of Your love (*benefit*). This we ask in Your name. Amen (*closing*).

When we use this type of organization for our prayers, we find four benefits. First, it focuses the thoughts of our prayer by helping us to organize our prayer from beginning to end. Second, it focuses us so that we do not stray from the things we feel a need to pray about and our prayers end up as a disconnected list of wishes and wants. Third, it helps us to meditate on the Scriptures as we pray. When we include a description of God or something He has done, we draw on what we know about Him from the Bible. Our prayer becomes a means of thinking about and applying what we have read in the Scriptures. Finally, following this or another pattern in prayer helps us make our prayers true prayers. That is, our prayers become spiritual exercises that keep us focused on what God has done for us as we learn it from His Word. Thereby, God's promises draw us closer to Him. That is what Jesus was teaching His disciples. When we learn to pray as Jesus taught His followers to pray, we stop going to God with a disjointed, rambling list of self-centered needs and requests, and our prayer becomes true prayer.

❋ Learning to Pray from Other Prayers in the Bible

The Lord's Prayer is not the only prayer in the Bible that serves as an example of prayer for us to imitate. Once we have learned the lessons that Jesus teaches us in the Lord's Prayer, we can search the Scriptures to find other examples to guide us as our prayer life grows and matures.

※ Ezra Reminds Us to Remember God's Promises When We Pray

In the Book of Ezra we find a short prayer that the people prayed when the temple's foundation was laid:

And they sang responsively, praising and giving
thanks to the Lord,
"For He is good, for His steadfast love
endures forever toward Israel." (3:11a)

This short prayer of praise contains two descriptions of God. It tells us that He is good and reminds us that God never does anything that is not good. Then it draws a conclusion about God—that His mercy endures forever. This prayer not only brought glory to God but also encouraged the people. As they praised God for His mercy, they were encouraging one another to rely on His mercy and to not lose heart when hardship or sorrow entered their life. This prayer was not new. It was part of the prayers when David brought the ark to Jerusalem (1 Chronicles 16:34, 41). It was sung again when Solomon dedicated the first temple in Jerusalem (2 Chronicles 7:3, 6). Through Jeremiah the Lord promised that it would be sung again in Jerusalem (Jeremiah 33:11). It also is the basis of Psalm 106, 107, 118, and 136.

This short prayer is an excellent example of a powerful prayer that has inspired God's people to pray and meditate. In Psalm 106 and 136 it serves as a framework for reviewing God's mercy throughout the Israelites' history. From this prayer, we learn that a short, well-crafted prayer can be as powerful as a long one. Our prayers are not heard because of the number of words we speak. They do not have to contain lofty phrases to touch the hearts of those who pray with us. This short prayer tells us that the content of prayer is all-important. This prayer points to a central truth about God—that He has promised to be merciful without limit. That alone has made it powerful.

When we pray, we need to learn to center our prayers on God's promises. That is what can make our prayers powerful in their effect on us and on others. We may not always choose eloquent words or be able to express all the thoughts of learned theologians. Nevertheless, our prayers can be moving and meaningful if they simply center on God's promises. That is what this one short biblical prayer did.

☀ Agur Teaches Us to Examine Our Lives before We Pray

Another short prayer that can teach us how to pray is Proverbs 30:7–9:

> Two things I ask of You;
>> deny them not to me before I die:
> Remove far from me falsehood
>> and lying;
>> give me neither poverty nor riches;
>> feed me with the food that is needful for me,

lest I be full and deny You

and say, "Who is the LORD?"

or lest I be poor and steal

and profane the name of my God.

This prayer by Agur is remarkable because it closely mirrors some of the thoughts in the Lord's Prayer, especially the fourth and sixth petitions. Agur's two requests of God are personal in nature. The first, much like the sixth petition of the Lord's Prayer, is a prayer that he would not be tempted. However, this request is more specific than the sixth petition. It requests that God would not allow Agur to be tempted to speak lies or other words intended to deceive people.

Agur's second request is that God would not allow him to become too poor or too rich. Agur explains that if he becomes too rich and can count on always having an abundance of food (and other possessions), he might be tempted to forget about God. He might think that he can get along without his Creator. If Agur becomes too poor, he might be tempted to steal to provide for his needs. This would reflect badly on God's name because Agur claims to be a follower of God. Therefore, Agur's second petition is not simply a request that God would give him his daily bread (the fourth petition of the Lord's Prayer). It is also a request that God would not allow circumstances to tempt him to sin and deny God (the sixth petition) or bring shame on God's name (the first petition).

Why did Agur pray for these two things? The answer to that question is in his explanation of his second request. Agur knew he was prone to certain types of sin. While we are all sinful, not all temptations are equally powerful for each person. One person may be more likely to commit one type of sin, whereas the temptation for another type of sin is more appealing to a different person. Agur understood his temptation to misuse wealth. He prayed that God would help him with that temptation.

Agur's prayer teaches us that we need to examine our lives before we pray. What are our needs? They may be different from the needs others feel. What are our strengths and weaknesses? They may not be the same strengths and weaknesses others have. When we pray with others, we may want to pray for a general deliverance from temptation. When we pray by ourselves, we should pray especially for those things that apply to ourselves.

However, to pray such prayers we need to learn about ourselves. We need to examine our lives and learn what spiritual challenges we face and need help in overcoming. Agur did that and could pray about his needs. We cannot pray as he did unless we take the time to understand ourselves and the spiritual struggles that we face every day. This is a difficult spiritual exercise because we often deny our faults and failures. We deny them so well that we overlook them. However, prayer becomes true prayer—spiritual exercise that draws us to God—when we have first examined ourselves in the light of God's Word as Agur did. Then we pray with trust in God's promises in the Scriptures as Ezra did.

※ Jesus Applied the Insights from Ezra and Agur in His Prayers

As we gain insights into ways of enhancing our prayers, we then need to apply those insights as we pray. It is not enough to learn some theoretical knowledge about prayer, we must also put that knowledge to work so it will not be lost. Most of us know this from personal experience. In high school or college we study many subjects that enable us to train for a career and to become a well-rounded person. However, in many cases we have forgotten much of the details of what we learned in subject areas we do not use often. Unless our career is in the area of life sciences, we probably have forgotten most of the details of our high school biology class. We may remember dissecting that frog, but most of us probably could not remember the chemical process by which DNA controls the development of an organism, the number of human chromosomes, or many other detailed topics we covered in biology class.

In the same way, we need to use the lessons we learn from the Bible's prayers if we are to retain them. One prayer of Jesus clearly shows us that He applied the lessons that can be drawn from Ezra's and Agur's prayers. It is the prayer of Jesus on the night before He was crucified (John 17:1–26). As Jesus opens His prayer, He speaks about His Father and Himself. This part of His prayer shows that Jesus understood Himself and what He had done in this world:

> Father, the hour has come; glorify Your Son that the Son may glorify You, since You have given Him authority over all flesh, to give eternal life to all whom You have given Him. And this is eternal life, that they know You the only true God, and Jesus Christ whom You have sent. I glorified You on earth, having accomplished the work that You gave me to do. And now, Father, glorify me in Your own presence with the glory that I had with You before the world existed.
>
> *(John 17:1b–5)*

Jesus' prayer goes on to make requests for others, but its foundation is this first section. It shows that Jesus clearly knew His needs and the things that He needed to do. He brought them to the Father in prayer. Jesus' prayer teaches us to do the same.

✳ A Word about the Prayer of Jabez

Recently much attention has been given to one of the Bible's shortest and most obscure prayers, the prayer said by Jabez.[4] All we know about Jabez is found in 1 Chronicles:

> Jabez was more honorable than his brothers; and his mother called his name Jabez, saying, "Because I bore him in pain." Jabez called upon the God of Israel, saying, "Oh that You would bless me and enlarge my border, and that Your hand might be with me, and that You would keep me from harm so that it might not bring me pain!" And God granted what he asked.
>
> *(4:9–10)*

A number of interesting but hard to translate terms are used in these two verses. The first is the play on words between the name *Jabez* (Hebrew *Y'abez*) and the word for *pain* or *distress* (Hebrew *'ozeb*), which was the source for his name. Apparently the name Jabez was a reminder of difficulties his mother had at the time he was born.

The word for *pain* or *distress* can refer to physical pain. Perhaps Jabez's mother had an especially painful delivery when Jabez was born. On the other hand, this word can signify a kind of psychological pain. Perhaps Jabez's mother was experiencing some type of additional trouble in her life when she went into labor and gave birth to him. Normally, we can tell the difference between these two meanings by context. However, because the account of Jabez and his birth are so short, we have virtually no clues from context to tell whether Jabez's mother was speaking of physical pain or psychological distress.

When we look at Jabez's prayer, we find that he asked God for blessing, which he defines in three ways:

1. That God would enlarge his borders.
2. That God's hand would be with him.
3. That God would keep him from harm/evil so that he would not be in pain/distress.

First, Jabez asked that God would "enlarge my border." This phrase sounds as if he is requesting that God give him more land. More land in Israel would have meant more prosperity and riches. If this is the case, there is an immediate problem. When the people of Israel were given the land of Canaan, each male head of a household was granted specific territory by God (Numbers 26:52–56). The land had to stay in the family from generation to generation. It could not be sold permanently. If it was sold, it was to be returned to the original family of owners every fifty years (Leviticus 25:10). Therefore, if Jabez's prayer was for more land (and, by implication, for riches), he was saying that he was not satisfied with the land God had set apart for him and that he wished to own property that God had intended for others. This is hardly the request of a man who was "more honorable than his brothers." Thus the first part of Jabez's prayer is not a prayer for prosperity.

Perhaps a clue to what Jabez was actually requesting is found in 1 Chronicles 2:55: "The clans also of the scribes who lived at Jabez: the Tirathites, the Shimeathites and the

Sucathites. These are the Kenites who came from Hammath, the father of the house of Rechab." It may be that the city or village of Jabez was named after the man who uttered the prayer in 1 Chronicles 4. Perhaps Jabez was praying that God would enlarge his borders by allowing his influence as a man of God to reach others. Perhaps God answered his prayer, and his influence was so great that a place was named after him.

Next, Jabez asked for God's hand to be with him. The explicit mention of God's hand being with someone is found only one other time in the Old Testament. In Psalm 89:21 we read that God promised David that His hand would be with David. This was a promise that God would support, strengthen, and bless David. A reading of Psalm 89 shows that while there were some physical blessings that came with this promise, the focus of the promise was on spiritual blessings. God would defend David from wicked men (Psalm 89:23), ensure him of His love (Psalm 89:25, 29), allow him to recognize God as his Father, God, and Savior (Psalm 89:27), and establish his throne forever (Psalm 89:30), a promise that is fulfilled in Jesus as David's son who rules forever in a kingdom where His people are forgiven their sins through His suffering, death, and resurrection. So it is most likely that Jabez also was focusing on *spiritual* blessings from God above physical blessings.

Finally, we come to Jabez's last request. This leads us to the other perplexing word in this prayer, the one that can mean either *harm* or *evil*. Once again, context often dictates what this word means. It can refer to physical, emotional, or psychological harm to an individual or a group without necessarily implying any moral judgment. However, it can also mean that some act that causes harm is against God's will and, therefore, is *evil*. Which is the case for Jabez's request? Given the context of Jabez's prayer to this point, we should suspect that this request also focuses on spiritual blessings. That is, Jabez was requesting that God keep him away from committing *evil* acts so that he would not be *distressed* by his sinful behavior. Jabez recognized that he was a sinner and needed God's power of forgiveness to overcome sin.

Thus when we take a close look at Jabez's prayer, we find that it reinforces many of the concepts we have already learned about prayer from other prayers in the Bible. In the first chapter we learned that *prayer does not begin with human effort to pester God until He listens. Prayer begins with God's promise of mercy toward us.* Jabez was an honorable man who understood this. His prayer relied on God's promises, and he prayed on the basis of those promises of spiritual blessing. We also learned in the first chapter that *prayer is not a way to manipulate God into answering all our questions or solve our problems in the ways we want them solved. Prayer is designed to help us transcend our problems and troubles by focusing on God Himself.* Jabez focused on God as the only true source of blessing. He did not try to manipulate God into giving him riches and prosperity, but he prayed for the spiritual blessings that God wants to shower on all His people.

In the second chapter we saw that *our prayers can be proactive. They can ask God for blessings and for good to come from what we do.* This is exactly what Jabez asked God, and God answered his prayer by "enlarging his borders." Further on in the third chapter we learned that *prayer can give us confidence that God will forgive because of who God is.* Jabez had this confidence, so he could ask to be kept from evil. In this way his prayer is like the petition in the Lord's Prayer that requests deliverance from evil, as we saw in chapter six.

Thus the prayer of Jabez reinforces what we have learned throughout our study of prayer. It was not powerful for Jabez because it was repeated day after day. In fact, there is no evidence from the Bible that Jabez prayed this prayer more than once. Nor is Jabez's prayer some sort of magic set of words that ensure riches and prosperity. On the contrary, Jabez focused on spiritual blessings rather than riches. Finally, we can see that Jabez's prayer has some common elements with all prayers in the Bible. While it was the prayer of a godly man and can serve as a good example of prayer for us, it is not a better or more powerful prayer than any other prayer in the Bible. Instead, like all the prayers in the Bible, its power comes from God's promise to bless His people and to listen to their prayers.

In this chapter we have learned many things about prayer. The Lord's Prayer is one example of a model prayer that teaches us how to pray. We have also discovered two important truths about prayer. First, we learned that *God's Word, the Scriptures, is the foundation upon which prayers are built.* In the Scriptures we learn about our relationship to God. When we examine ourselves against their teachings, we can learn the personal spiritual challenges that we face so we can pray to God about the things we really need. Second, we learned that *we need to center our prayers on God's promises.* No matter how much self-examination we do, only God's promises can give us the assurance that we are His beloved children and move us to pray. When we apply these lessons about prayer, our prayers become real prayers.

><+>-O-<+><

Any number of prayers in the Bible can serve as guides for our own prayers. I would suggest Psalm 18, 25, 26, 42, 61, 72, 119 (the longest prayer in the Bible), and 141.

7

When God Receives Praise

Children require much attention and have an endless supply of requests. They rely on parents, grandparents, teachers, and others to supply them with the physical, emotional, and spiritual support and guidance they need to grow into mature adults. If parents do their job correctly, their children learn to be thankful for the things others do for them. When they are young, we have to train children to say "Thank you" to someone who has given them something or done them a favor. As they grow older, children learn to realize they should be thankful and learn how to express that thanks without having to be reminded. Expressing thanks is expected of those who understand the favors others have done for them.

Although we teach our children to thank others, we do not often teach them another equally important practice—praising others. Even as adults we find it difficult to praise a person who has done something well because it makes us feel a little uncomfortable. We are much more likely to praise them to others, though the persons who are being praised often do not hear it. Therefore, children seldom praise their parents for what they have done in providing a home and an education for them. This is unfortunate because giving well-deserved praise is an important way of showing how deeply grateful we are for the dedication and excellence others have brought to their responsibilities or obligations.

This reluctance to praise can lead to a deficit in our prayers. We may praise God less in our prayers than we ought. Like children who know to thank their parents but are reluctant to praise them, we can become people who thank God for what He does but fall short of praising Him. Thanks and praise go together. However, praise goes beyond gratitude for what God has done to recognition of the unsurpassed excellence of everything God does. It not only shows our gratitude but also shows our appreciation for God's nature and His works.

Prayers of praise in the Bible fall into two broad types. One is praise for God that urges others to also praise Him. The other type is praise that glorifies God's attributes or actions. Many prayers contain both of these types. As we examine both types of praise we will learn two important lessons: *We can and should praise God for the many things that He is and does. However, the greatest motivation for our praise for God comes from His love and compassion for us in His Son. Since our entire relationship with God is founded upon Christ, our praises always build upon His work for us.*

※ Psalm 150—Calling on Everyone to Praise God in Every Way

Praise the LORD!

Praise God in His sanctuary,

praise Him in His mighty heavens!

Praise Him for His mighty deeds;

praise Him according to His excellent

greatness!

Praise Him with trumpet sound;

praise Him with lute and harp!

Praise Him with tambourine and dance;

praise Him with strings and pipe!

Praise Him with sounding cymbals;

praise Him with loud clashing cymbals!

Let everything that has breath praise the LORD!

Praise the LORD!

This psalm (like Psalm 111–113, 135, and 146–149) begins by calling on God's people to praise Him. However, this is not the ordinary way for calling on someone to praise God. The word *hallelujah* (translated here as "Praise the LORD") is a combination of two Hebrew words: *Hallelu* (praise) and *Yah* (the shortened form of God's name, *Yahweh*). The word *hallelujah* occurs only in the Book of Psalms. This way of calling on people to praise God is reserved for worship. It specifically speaks to God's people gathered to worship Him. Therefore, it calls for praise for God from those who understand His mercy and goodness toward them.

Except for the beginning and ending hallelujahs, this psalm consists of ten sentences calling on people to praise God. The first one calls on people in His holy place to praise Him. That is, it calls on the people assembled in the temple to sing His praises in worship. The second one calls on everyone in heaven to praise Him. Thus all of God's people, not only those we see around us, but all those who have gone before us, are urged to praise Him.

Sentences three and four are the only two in this psalm that give a reason for praising God, and they do that in the most general of terms. We are urged to praise Him for who He is and for what He has done. This prayer does not elaborate on what God has done nor does it dwell on any particular attribute of God for which we are to praise Him. It leaves those things to the worshipers to contemplate. They may think of things He has done for them as a group. Or they may contemplate the many different things God has done for them as individuals. They may praise Him for all of His wonderful attributes, His power, knowledge, wisdom, glory, and so forth, or for particular attributes that they appreciate at the moment of praise.

The next lines urge us to praise God in a particular way—with music and dance. Among the musical instruments mentioned are trumpets, harps, tambourines, lutes, and cymbals, along with various stringed instruments. This psalm reminds us that prayers can be sung as well as spoken. Hymns often serve the function of prayers sung by groups of worshipers.

Since ancient times, God's people have used music as an important part of their worship of Him. Christians have always employed music in their worship, composing hymns in each generation, and handing the best of them down to the generations that followed. Part of that musical tradition has been praying to God in song, often accompanied by instruments. This ancient prayer of praise reminds us that some of our most important prayers make use of a marvelous gift that God has given to human beings—music. It reminds us that we use not only our minds and our folded hands[5] to praise God in our prayers, but that we also use our entire bodies, including our vocal cords. Musicians who lead the sung prayers may use their arms and hands, legs and feet, lips, mouth, and breath in praise to God (see the last line of the psalm). Those who sing may use their bodies as they stand or kneel. During prayer we can and should use our body to praise God, and we should use the great gift of music as part of our praises. During my times of prayer I have often found that singing a hymn to God is a powerful way to praise Him and come to Him in prayer, even when I am alone. This psalm urges us to make use of the gift of music as part of our regular practice of prayer.

However, music in worship and prayer is not an end in itself. While music has the power to beautify our prayers and deeply touch our souls, it is no substitute for the content of our prayer. That is why the psalmist urges God's people to praise Him for His works and His greatness before He encourages them to praise Him with music. Music for its own sake is not praise for God. Music with a message about our God and all He has done for us is.

Psalm 148—Calling on All Creation to Praise God

Praising God with music is only part of the message of the Bible's prayers of praise. Psalm 148 gives us another view of praise for God.

> Praise the LORD!
> Praise the LORD from the heavens;
>   praise Him in the heights!

Praise Him, all His angels;
    praise Him, all His hosts!
Praise Him, sun and moon,
    praise Him, all you shining stars!
Praise Him, you highest heavens,
    and you waters above the heavens!
Let them praise the name of the LORD!
    For He commanded and they were created.
And He established them forever and ever;
    He gave a decree, and it shall not pass away.
Praise the LORD from the earth,
    you great sea creatures and all deeps,
fire and hail, snow and mist,
    stormy wind fulfilling His word!
Mountains and all hills,
    fruit trees and all cedars!
Beasts and all livestock,
    creeping things and flying birds!
Kings of the earth and all peoples,
    princes and all rulers of the earth!
Young men and maidens together,
    old men and children!
Let them praise the name of the LORD,
    for His name alone is exalted;
    His majesty is above earth and heaven.

He has raised up a horn for His people,

praise for all His saints,

for the people of Israel who are near to Him.

Praise the LORD!

Like Psalm 150, the praise for God in this psalm consists mostly of calls for others to praise God. The first part calls on everything in the heavens to praise God. Not only are God's heavenly creatures, the angels, called on to give God praise but also heavenly bodies and even the clouds in the sky are encouraged to praise God. That may seem a little strange to us. We can identify with choirs of angels praising God in heaven, but how do the sun, moon, and stars praise God? Yet the concept of God receiving praise from His creation is not isolated to this psalm. Psalm 19:1–4 tells us:

The heavens declare the glory of God,

and the sky above proclaims His handiwork.

Day to day pours out speech,

and night to night reveals knowledge.

There is no speech, nor are there words,

whose voice is not heard.

Their measuring line goes out through all

the earth,

and their words to the end of the world.

God's creation tells of His glory and praises Him without having to say a word. When we contemplate the starry skies at night, when we marvel at the wonders of the universe that God created, we cannot help but think of His glory. Silently the clouds roll overhead, and the sun, stars, and moon pass by. Yet their testimony to God who placed them in the heavens and controls their movements is as loud as any praise God receives. In fact, that is why Psalm 148 calls on us to praise God: He created the heavens and He controls everything that happens in them.

The psalm moves on to call on the earth to praise God. The ocean and its creatures, the weather and its powerful storms, the mountains, plants, and animals are all told to praise God. This part of God's creation also testifies to His power and glory. All of these things should remind us of God's glory. The weather, which we can (sometimes) predict but cannot control, reminds us of God's might with every powerful storm. The wonderful, yet delicate, balance of animal and plant life that we can so easily destroy through environmental mismanagement reminds us of God's wisdom in ordering our world better than we can. He deserves our praise, and observation of His world should tell us that.

But the psalm does not stop with the other creatures around us. It calls on us to praise God. It calls on important people—kings, officials, judges—as well as all others to praise God. Moreover, it tells us to praise God for two reasons. One is His glory to which heaven and earth testify every day, as the psalm has already reminded us.

The other reason is that God has "raised up a horn for His people," meaning that He has given His people a powerful leader and defender. The Hebrew word for *horn* is often used to signify power in the Scriptures. Many animals, such as sheep, goats, cattle, and deer use their horns as part of their power to defend themselves and their young. The psalm uses the horn as a figure of speech to symbolize the strength God gives to His people. In Psalm 132:7 the horn is used as a symbol of a leader to come from King David's family. Here it is used to speak of a powerful leader for God's people.

The Gospel of Mark recognizes the "horn" spoken of in Psalm 148 as Jesus. Mark tells us that when Jesus rode into Jerusalem on the first Palm Sunday, the people shouted: "Hosanna in the highest!" (Mark 11:10). The Greek phrase for "in the highest heaven" matches the ancient Greek translation of the Old Testament in only one place—Psalm 148:1. Christians recognize that the strong leader God gives His people is Jesus, the horn from David's family. Therefore, Psalm 148 calls on the people of God, God's true Israel (Galatians 6:16), those who are close to Him by faith, to praise Him because of the work of the promised Savior.

This final emphasis in Psalm 148 leads us to an important principle about prayers of praise. *We can and should praise God for the many things that He is and does. However, the greatest motivation for our praise for God comes from His love and compassion for us in His Son.*

 Psalm 111 and the Books of Revelation and Daniel—Praising God for Who He Is and What He Does

Praise for God's love and compassion shown in His saving work for us is found in a number of psalms. One example is Psalm 111.

Praise the LORD!

I will give thanks to the LORD with my

whole heart,

in the company of the upright, in the

congregation.

Great are the works of the LORD,

studied by all who delight in them.

Full of splendor and majesty is His work,

and His righteousness endures forever.

He has caused His wondrous works to be

remembered;

the LORD is gracious and merciful.

He provides food for those who fear Him;

He remembers His covenant forever.

He has shown His people the power of

His works,

in giving them the inheritance

of the

nations.

The works of His hands are faithful and just;

all His precepts are trustworthy.

they are established forever and ever,

to be performed with faithfulness and

uprightness.

He sent redemption to His people;

He has commanded His covenant forever.

Holy and awesome is His name!

The fear of the LORD is the beginning

of wisdom;

all those who practice it have a good

understanding.

His praise endures forever!

Unlike the first two prayers of praise we have considered, this psalm does not consist mainly of calling on others to praise God. Instead, it consists of praise that glorifies God and His attributes. It starts with a brief thanks to God and continues with praise for the many things God does and is. Psalm 111 praises God for His great and wondrous works, including the miracles He has done. It praises God for providing for the daily needs of His people, especially their food. It praises Him for His truth and justice, especially for the principles that He gave to His people to guide them. All of these are important reasons for praising God and should be part of our praise to Him.

However, we should notice that woven throughout the praises in this psalm is praise for God's love, mercy, and compassion in saving us. Verse 4 describes God as merciful and compassionate. Verse 9 reminds us that He sends salvation to His people. And twice, in verses 5 and 9, this psalm reminds us that God keeps His promises, the foremost of which was His promise to send the Savior into the world. Like Psalm 148, this psalm centers its praise on God's compassion for His people.

When we turn to the pages of the New Testament, we find the praise for God's mercy in Jesus is seen even more clearly in the praises in Revelation. In the fifth chapter where

Jesus is introduced as the Lamb, we read a prayer of praise offered by God's people in heaven.

> Worthy are You to take the scroll
>> and to open its seals,
> for You were slain, and by Your blood
>> You ransomed people for God
> from every tribe and language and people
>> and nation,
> and You have made them a kingdom and
>> priests to our God,
> and they shall reign on the earth.
>> *(Revelation 5:9–10)*

This praise centers squarely on Jesus' sacrifice on the cross. He is praised because He died. The praise then further builds because of the consequences of Jesus' death on the cross. His blood bought people from all over the world to be God's own. This praise gives Jesus all the credit for bringing people to God. We cannot claim to have contributed anything to our status before God as His people because Christ did all the work. Nor can we praise ourselves for the status we have in God's sight as members of His kingdom and as priests who serve Him (see Exodus 19:6; 1 Peter 2:9). Jesus made us these by His sacrifice. Even the final sentence: "They shall reign on the earth," is really praise for Jesus because it is His work that makes us royalty.

Two more prayers follow this praise. These also direct us to Jesus' death on the cross as the major reason for our praise for God:

"Worthy is the Lamb who was slain, to receive power and wealth and wisdom and might and honor and glory and blessing!"

(Revelation 5:12)

"To Him who sits on the throne and to the Lamb be blessing and honor and glory and might forever and ever!"

(Revelation 5:13)

The last of these prayers is especially important. This is praise for Jesus because He was the lamb who was offered as a sacrifice for the whole world. But this is also praise for God the Father (the one on the throne). He was willing to give up His Son to a horrible death so we could have life. Both the Father and the Son share the praise for the compassion and mercy they showed us at the cross on Calvary.

How different these prayers of praise are from those we are often tempted to pray. We usually praise God for the good things He does for us in this life. When something happens in our life that we consider good—restoration of health, a new job or promotion, the birth of a child, the marriage of a son or daughter—we might find an occasion to praise God. These are proper things to praise God for. However, they pale in comparison to the death of Christ for us. If our praise to God is *only* for things in this life, it is not much in the way of praise.

After all, Paul reminds us: "If in this life only we have hoped in Christ, we are of all people most to be pitied" (1 Corinthians 15:19). However, if our praise is coupled with our praise to God for saving us from sin and death, if our praises for things in this life presuppose and build upon praise for Christ's sacrifice on the cross, then we have learned how to pray true biblical praises.

The praises in Revelation build on the cross of Christ. In chapter 15 we find another prayer of praise. It is the praise of all who win the victory over evil.

> Great and amazing are Your deeds,
>> O Lord God the Almighty!
> Just and true are Your ways,
>> O King of the nations!
> Who will not fear, O Lord,
>> and glorify Your name?
> For You alone are holy.
> All nations will come and worship You,
> for Your righteous acts have been revealed.
>> *(15:3–4)*

God's "righteous acts" in the last verse is not primarily referring to judgment against sin and sinners, a judgment of condemnation. Instead, it is a reference to God's judgment of acquittal of sinners for Jesus' sake. It is speaking about God's judgment that sets aside our well-deserved punishment because Jesus has suffered our punishment for us on the cross. God's judgment and the work of His Son are the spectacular and amazing things to which this prayer refers. His decision to give us life through Christ is what is praised as fair and true. And that is why people fear Him and come to worship Him.

Thus while this prayer of praise does not specifically mention the work of Christ, it is built upon it. Our praises should be built on that same foundation. Sometimes they will explicitly mention the work of Christ to free us from sin. Other times they may presuppose it as their foundation. This is a lesson about prayer we should always remember: *Since our entire relationship with God is founded upon Christ, our praises always build upon His work for us.*

In this light we can understand the prayers of praise in the Bible. One example is the prayer of Daniel when God gave him the ability to tell King Nebuchadnezzar what the king had dreamt and what it meant. Nebuchadnezzar had threatened Daniel with execution if he could not tell him. When Daniel was shown the dream and its interpretation, the first thing he did was to praise God. He could have chosen to go to the king and tell him the dream, then, after the danger had passed, praise God. Instead, Daniel praised God first. His faith in God who through the coming Savior would make him part of the eternal kingdom of God (Daniel 2:44–45) caused him to praise God before doing anything else. That prayer, Daniel 2:20–23, praises God for His wisdom and power.

Blessed be the name of God forever and ever,

    to whom belong wisdom and might.

He changes times and seasons;

    He removes kings and sets up kings;

He gives wisdom to the wise

and knowledge to those who have
understanding;
He reveals deep and hidden things;
He knows what is in the darkness,
and the light dwells with Him.
To You, O God of my fathers,
I give thanks and praise,
for You have given me wisdom and might,
and have now made known to me what we
asked of You,
for You have made known to us the
king's matter.

God gave Daniel wisdom so he could tell the king what he wanted to know. Daniel's wisdom, however, was greater than knowing how to interpret a dream. It was a Christ-centered wisdom that led him to praise God.

✳ The Song of the Three—How God's People in the Past Learned to Praise Him

The examples of biblical prayers we have seen in this chapter have taught us how to praise God in our prayers. That lesson was also learned by the people of long ago. As I close this chapter I would like to offer another prayer composed by God's people. This prayer is found in the ancient Greek version of Daniel. Although it is not part of the original Hebrew and Aramaic, it is nevertheless a wonderful prayer of praise to

God. In Greek it comes immediately after the three young men, Shadrach, Meshach, and Abednego (also known by their Hebrew names Hananiah, Azariah, and Mishael) were thrown into the blazing furnace for refusing King Nebuchadnezzar's order to worship an idol (see Daniel 3). The ancient writer of this prayer, called the Song of the Three, imagined these young men praising God in the midst of the fire as God's angel protected them from the flames. This prayer draws on many of the praises to God found in the Old Testament. It shows us that from ancient times God's people learned to pray by reading and studying the prayers in the Bible.

You are praised, Lord God of our ancestors,

and You are worthy of praise and supreme

honor forever.

Moreover, Your glorious and holy name is praised

and it is worthy of supreme praise

and supreme honor

throughout every age.

You are praised in the temple where Your

holy glory is,

and You are to be supremely praised

with songs and

supremely glorified forever.

You are praised as You look into the depths

of the earth as You sit on the angels,[6]

and You are worthy of praise and to be

glorified forever.

You are praised as You are on the throne of Your kingdom,

   and You are to be praised with songs

      and supreme honor forever.

You are praised in the sky,

   and You are to be praised with songs

      and glorified forever.

All things that the Lord has done, praise the Lord.

   Sing His praise and give Him supreme honor forever.

Heavens, praise the Lord.

   Sing His praise and give Him supreme honor forever.

All angels of the Lord, praise the Lord.

   Sing His praise and give Him supreme honor forever.

Water above the heavens, praise the Lord.

   Sing His praise and give Him supreme honor forever.

All powers of the Lord, praise the Lord.

   Sing His praise and give Him supreme honor forever.

Sun and moon, praise the Lord.

   Sing His praise and give Him supreme honor forever.

Stars in heaven, praise the Lord.

   Sing His praise and give Him supreme honor forever.

Thunderstorms and dew, praise the Lord.

   Sing His praise and give Him supreme honor forever.

All winds, praise the Lord.

   Sing His praise and give Him supreme honor forever.

Fire and heat, praise the Lord.

Sing His praise and give Him supreme honor forever.

Winter's cold and summer's heat, praise the Lord.

Sing His praise and give Him supreme honor forever.

Frost and cold weather, praise the Lord.

Sing His praise and give Him supreme honor forever.

Dew and snow, praise the Lord.

Sing His praise and give Him supreme honor forever.

Nights and days, praise the Lord.

Sing His praise and give Him supreme honor forever.

Light and darkness, praise the Lord.

Sing His praise and give Him supreme honor forever.

Ice crystals and falling snow, praise the Lord.

Sing His praise and give Him supreme honor forever.

Flashes of lightning and clouds, praise the Lord.

Sing His praise and give Him supreme honor forever.

Earth, praise the Lord.

Sing His praise and give Him supreme honor forever.

Mountains and hills, praise the Lord.

Sing His praise and give Him supreme honor forever.

Everything that grows in the ground, praise the Lord.

Sing His praise and give Him supreme honor forever.

Seas and rivers, praise the Lord.

Sing His praise and give Him supreme honor forever.

Springs, praise the Lord.

Sing His praise and give Him supreme honor forever.

Whales and everything that swims in water,

praise the Lord.

Sing His praise and give Him supreme honor forever.

Every bird in the air, praise the Lord.

Sing His praise and give Him supreme honor forever.

All wild animals and cattle, praise the Lord.

Sing His praise and give Him supreme honor forever.

All people, praise the Lord.

Sing His praise and give Him supreme honor forever.

Israel, praise the Lord.

Sing His praise and give Him supreme honor forever.

Priests, praise the Lord.

Sing His praise and give Him supreme honor forever.

Servants of the Lord, praise the Lord.

Sing His praise and give Him supreme honor forever.

Spirits and souls of those who have His approval,

praise the Lord.

Sing His praise and give Him supreme honor forever.

Holy people and those who are sincerely humble,

praise the Lord.

Sing His praise and give Him supreme honor forever.

Hananiah, Azariah and Mishael, praise the Lord.

Sing His praise and give Him supreme honor forever

because He has rescued us from hell.

He has saved us from the power of death

He has released us from the blazing flames

and freed us from the fire.

Give thanks to the Lord because He is good,

because His mercy endures forever.

Everyone who worships the God of Gods,

sing His praise and thank Him

because His mercy endures forever and ever.

(Daniel 3:52–90,
author's translation)

For more than two thousand years God's people have learned to offer Him prayers of praise by reading the Bible and adapting its praises. We can grow in this aspect of our prayer life by doing the same.

>—+—+>—0—<+—+—<

The Book of Psalms contains many prayers of praise. I would recommend that for additional study you begin with the last group of psalms, those that begin and end with *hallelujah*. Of those, Psalm 146, 147, and 149 have not been treated in this chapter.

8

Making Prayer a Part
of Your Life

In the previous seven chapters we have looked at the Bible's
prayers for desperate times and prosperous times, times of
trial and temptation, and times of joy. What we have not done
is look at what the Bible says about prayer. Instead, we have
looked at actual prayers and learned from them important
lessons to guide us as we pray. In this last chapter I want to
offer some suggestions for further Bible study on the topic of
prayer. These suggestions can help you grow in your understanding of and in your practice of prayer.

A number of approaches to studying prayer in the Bible
can be fruitful. The use of a concordance[7] will be helpful. Look
up words such as *pray, prayer, thank, thanksgiving, song, hymn,*
and *praise.* However, finding these words will not necessarily make for a good study of prayer in the Bible. In the New
Testament alone these words occur in more than 150 verses.
Your study will have to be sharpened and narrowed to make

progress in studying what the Bible says about prayer. After you find them, you may want to study them in groups:

1. Study those passages that are instructions on how to pray, when to pray, what to pray for, and so on. For instance, Jesus teaches about prayer in Matthew 5:44 and 6:5–18. Paul tells his readers to pray in Ephesians 6:18–20 and Colossians 4:2–4.

2. Study passages that tell us about people in the Bible praying. Many of these do not include the prayers themselves, but they tell us when and why God's people in the past prayed. From their examples we can learn much about prayer. Look for when, how, and why people prayed. If you include study of words such as *thank* and *praise,* you can learn about special types of prayer while studying these passages. In addition, a few passages serve as negative examples, showing us how not to pray (Mark 12:40).

3. Study passages that describe prayers offered by God's people. Paul often describes his prayers (see Romans 1:9; Ephesians 1:16–23; Philippians 1:3–11). Others also describe their prayers or the prayers of others. These descriptions are valuable in helping us to understand not only what Christians in the past have prayed about but also why they prayed. We can receive insight into their motivations to pray and their reflections about the prayers they prayed.

4. Continue to study prayers in the Bible. This is perhaps the most difficult way to study prayer in the Bible, but I believe that it is the most rewarding. By studying the actual prayers of the Bible we are forced to ask questions such as: Why was this prayer prayed? When was it prayed? How do the prayer's various parts work together to bring the concerns of the person praying before God? Are several concerns or topics evident in this prayer, and how do they relate to one another?

These questions are often automatically answered for us in the first three ways to study prayer in the Bible that I have listed. Only by studying the prayers in the Bible are we forced to wrestle with the setting, occasion, and content of the prayer. When studying many of the psalms, we can only guess at the setting or occasion of the prayer from studying its contents. In other cases, the setting and occasion are given, but studying the prayer itself will give us a better appreciation for them. In addition, only by studying actual prayers in the Bible can we discover various ways of composing and structuring our prayers.

As you study prayers, keep in mind some of the most important lessons we have learned. Prayer from beginning to end is dependent on God and His promises. As Christians we acknowledge that we can only understand the promises of God by knowing Jesus Christ and what He has done for us in His life, death, and resurrection.

Finally, practice constructing prayers from the examples in the Bible. Use the concepts, words, phrases, and even sentences of biblical prayers and incorporate them in your prayers. Learn about the occasions that prompted others to pray, and pray in similar circumstances in your life. Moreover, learn to use all of your Bible study to guide you in prayer. We can use everything we learn in the Bible, even when we are not specifically studying about prayer, to guide us to offer richer, more effective prayers. As you do these things, God will guide you by His Word so you will be able to make prayer an essential and regular part of your life.

This approach to a growing prayer life has enriched my life. It has opened up all of the Scriptures as a resource for my prayers. I can include a wide variety of the thoughts, words, and phrases provided by God Himself in the Bible. Moreover, it enables me to avoid becoming bored and tired of my own prayers. Instead, I can constantly incorporate the new insights God provides as I read the Scriptures and meditate on their potential to teach me how to pray. This is especially important for me because as a pastor I am often called upon to pray with others and to lead them in prayer. However, you do not need to be a pastor to apply this book's lessons to your life. All you need is a Bible and a desire to learn the lessons it teaches us in the prayers recorded in its pages.

Endnotes

1. The Large Catechism, in *The Book of Concord*, ed. Robert Kolb and Timothy Wengert (Minneapolis: Augsburg, 2000), 401.

2. The Ten Commandments are numbered in two different ways. (The Bible never numbers the commandments.) The numbering I am using counts three commandments in Exodus 20:1–7 (or its repetition in Deuteronomy 5:6–15) and seven commandments in Exodus 20:8–17 (or its repetition in Deuteronomy 5:16–21) (counting verse 17 as two commands against sinful desires). The alternate numbering counts four commandments in Exodus 20:1–7 (counting verses 3 and 4 as separate commands) and six commandments in Exodus 20:8–17.

3. Although the closing of the Lord's Prayer is included in the familiar King James Version of the Bible (first published in 1611), it is not present in the oldest Greek manuscripts of Matthew and is not present in any manuscript of Luke. Among the manuscripts of Matthew that do include it, its wording varies considerably. The words themselves do not come from Jesus but are based on Solomon's prayer at the dedication of the temple (1 Chronicles 29:11–13). The closing was probably added in an attempt to make the prayer come to a less abrupt ending when used in worship.

4. This prayer has been popularized mainly through Bruce Wilkinson's book, *The Prayer of Jabez: Breaking Through to the Blessed Life.*

5. While the most common custom in the modern Western world is to fold hands while praying, the ancient practice was to lift up arms and hands during praying. (For example, see Psalm 28:2 or 63:4.)

6. Or "cherubim."

7. A concordance is an alphabetical list of words that occur in the Bible. Under each word are listed occurrences of the word by book, chapter, and verse. Often a short context line includes a portion of the verse in which the word occurs to help you see how it is used. Some Bibles include short concordances in the back. Longer, complete Bible concordances are available in bookstores and libraries.

Prayers in the Bible

This list includes all of the prayers studied in this book as well as many of the prayers in the Bible outside of the Book of Psalms.

Chapter 1—When God Seems Deaf

Chapter 2—When Evil Is Winning

Numbers 11:10–15	Moses' complaint
2 Samuel 15:31	Make Ahithophel's advice foolish
Nehemiah 5:19	Remember me, my God . . .
Nehemiah 6:14	Remember my enemies
Nehemiah 13:14, 22, 31	Remember me . . .
Psalm 137	By the waters of Babylon
Jeremiah 11:20	Prayer for revenge by God
Jeremiah 17:12–18	Prayer for revenge by God
Jeremiah 18:19–23	Prayer for revenge by God
Jeremiah 20:7–18	Jeremiah's complaint
Habakkuk 1:2–4	Habakkuk's prayer for justice
Habakkuk 1:12–17	Habakkuk's prayer for justice against Babylon
Habakkuk 3:1–19	
Acts 4:24–30	Prayer about persecution
Acts 7:60	Stephen's prayer for his killers

Chapter 3—When Sin Is Recognized

Ezra 9:6–15	Ezra's prayer for the people
Nehemiah 1:5–10	Nehemiah's prayer about Jerusalem
Daniel 9:4–19	Daniel's prayer about Jerusalem

Chapter 4—When Health Fails

2 Kings 20:3	Hezekiah's prayer to live (Isaiah 38:3)
Luke 23:46	Father, into Your hands

Chapter 5—When Family Provides Support

1 Samuel 1:10–13	Hannah's prayer for a child

Chapter 6—When Prayer Becomes True Prayer

Ezra 3:11	He is good, His mercy endures forever
Proverbs 30:7–9	Ask for two things
Matthew 6:9–13	Our Father (Luke 22:42)
Luke 23:34	Father, forgive them
John 17:1–26	High Priestly Prayer

Chapter 7—When God Receives Praise

1 Samuel 2:1–10	Hannah's prayer of thanks
Daniel 2:20–23	Daniel's prayer of thanks

Other Prayers to Study

Genesis 24:12–14	Abraham's servant
Deuteronomy 3:23–25	Moses' request to see the Promised Land
Joshua 7:7–9	Prayer after the defeat at Ai
2 Samuel 7:18–29	David prays about God's promise (2 Chronicles 17:16–27)
1 Kings 8:22–53	Dedication of the temple (2 Chronicles 6:12–42, Psalm 132:1, 8–10)
1 Kings 17:21	Elijah prays for dead child's life
1 Chronicles 16:8–36	Ark brought to Jerusalem (Psalm 96, 105, 106)

1 Chronicles 29:10–19	David's praise at the offerings for the temple
Nehemiah 9:5–37	Day of prayer
Jeremiah 32:16–25	Jeremiah prays for Jerusalem
Jonah 2:2–9	Jonah's prayer from the fish
Matthew 26:39–42	(Mark 14:36; Luke 22:42)
Luke 1:46–55	Magnificat
Luke 2:29–32	Nunc Dimitis
Acts 1:24–25	Prayer for Judas's replacement
Revelation 22:20b	Come, Lord Jesus

Index of Scripture Citations

	PAGE
Psalms, *continued*	
119	144
127:3–5	100
128	99, 107–112
129	50
130	55, 62–63
132:7	155
133	99, 112–116
135	149
136	135
137	29–33
140	50
141	144
143	55, 73
146	149, 167
147	149, 167
148	149, 151–153
148:1	155
149	149, 167
150	148–151, 153
Proverbs	
3:12	120
25:1	78
30:7–9	136–138
Isaiah	
38:9–20	78
39:1–8	78
Jeremiah	
11:20	33
17:18	34
33:11	135

CPSIA information can be obtained at www.ICGtesting.com
Printed in the USA
LVOW122052221211

260801LV00001B/7/P